THE
GREENHOUSE
EFFECT

THE GREENHOUSE EFFECT

Eric Swanson

LITTLE, BROWN AND COMPANY

BOSTON   TORONTO   LONDON

Library of Congress Cataloging-in-Publication Data

Swanson, Eric.
    The greenhouse effect / Eric Swanson.
        p.   cm.
    ISBN 0-316-82477-1
    I. Title.
PS3569.W2685G74   1990
813'.54 — dc20   89-13637
                                              CIP

10 9 8 7 6 5 4 3 2 1

FG

Published simultaneously in Canada
by Little, Brown & Company (Canada) Limited

Printed in the United States of America

This book is for Emma Sweeney

Another world do I hold in mind . . .
— Gottfried von Strassburg,
Tristan und Isold

PART ONE

1

THIS IS HOW IT STARTS. A fire engine goes by, blasting its horn. Another passes; then another. A three-alarm fire in the middle of a hot day. The thought of it makes me dizzy for a minute. All that disaster. People on the sidewalks cover their ears. Cars pull to a stop at the side of the road. I notice as the trucks go by that some of the firemen are smiling. They seem very relaxed about where they're going, even pleased, and it's not just for show. Those smiles are genuine. At the same time, I think, they have to know what they're getting into; they have to realize that.

The kid next to me says, Choose.

What?

Choose to have things, he says. And they'll be yours. You get what you choose.

Really? I say. Isn't that funny.

It is tremendously hot out, well over a hundred degrees, and, all around, the exhaust from cars and buses hangs thickly in the air, trembling, like some strange transparent beast. The sky above is a dull gray-white, and the awful heat makes everything present and terribly real. It's not easy weather for pretending.

What's your name? I ask the kid.

Christopher, he says.

Nice to meet you, Christopher, I say.

Nice to meet you, he says.

I'd seen him staring into the window of a store as I was coming down Eighth Avenue from the park. He was shorter than me, and skinnier, with light wavy hair. He'd turned and smiled when he saw that I was watching him. I didn't realize how young he was until I was standing right next to him, and then it was too late; the damage was already done. There was nothing to do but play it out.

He couldn't have been more than seventeen or eighteen. I was embarrassed by that, and I stared hard into the store window at a display of candlesticks and metal bowls painted with something to make them look green and weathered. I made a dumb remark about wanting to have things; it was so banal that I was even more embarrassed. Then the fire trucks went by, and after they passed I realized that I was soaked with sweat; I was embarrassed by that, too.

The kid was as affected by the heat as anyone. His hair was sticking to his face, and lines of sweat ran down his arms. But he put his arm around my shoulder, and my heart started to beat fast. Neither of us said anything. We looked in the window some more, and I shifted once to glance at him next to me. His pupils were dilated. I wondered if he was on something. He saw me looking at him.

Do you wanna walk? he asked.

All right, I said. Sure.

We kicked off from the side of the building and walked to the corner. He kept his arm around me as we crossed the street. We went down Fifty-seventh Street, towards Ninth Avenue.

You from around here? I asked him.

South of here, he said. Way south.

Why are you here? I asked.

He shrugged.

No good reason, he said. I just wanted to.

Good enough, I said.

He pulled away from me and took a few steps ahead, so as to face me directly.

Can you do this? he asked, circling his head in such a way as to look like he wasn't moving his neck at all. It looked like his head was moving on some kind of ball bearing.

I replied that I couldn't.

Can you do this? he asked.

He started bending his fingers in weird directions, each time asking me if I could do the same thing. Finally I told him that I wasn't a demonstrative type of person, I wasn't flexible at all. He seemed to like that; anyway, it made him smile. He stopped doing tricks and fell into place next to me again. The heat closed down around us. I wondered if it would rain.

On the corner of Ninth and Fifty-seventh, a couple of old drunk men were sleeping in a concrete public space, their shirts open, flies buzzing around their mouths and scabby legs. Some pigeons were holding parliament in the shade of the Parc Vendome. An old Korean woman, her spine twisted and humpy with scoliosis, seemed to tiptoe down the street toward us, pulling a wire grocery cart behind her. Further down Ninth, children ran around in a stream of water pouring out of a fire hydrant, while a couple of grown-ups sat watching them on a stoop.

We turned south. Smoke from the fire further down Fifty-seventh rose black and billowy over the tops of buildings. It was close enough to smell, acrid and sooty. When we got down to Fifty-first Street, I asked the kid if he

wanted to come up, and he said yes, so we turned west and
walked the half block to my apartment building. Two His-
panic guys were sitting on the front steps, drinking beer. I
nodded to them. They nodded back, and shifted to let us
step up between them. I unlocked the front door and let the
kid in ahead of me. The walls in the hallway were covered
in a red and black vinyl that was supposed to look like
paneling. I was used to it after ten years, but I wondered
what the kid might think. That was an old habit. I didn't
know this kid, yet I was concerned about what he might
think of the wallpaper.

He ran his finger across it as he walked down the hall,
without comment.

My apartment was on the second floor. When we got inside,
I opened both windows as far as they would go and turned
on the fan. I didn't own an air conditioner. Most of the time
I was just as happy with the arrangement. This summer
was an exception. This summer, there was no getting
around the heat, and no living with it. Fire had arrived out
of nowhere, right at the beginning of the season, and
burned over heaven, pressing down harder every day. Each
day everyone was a little more worn out. It might have been
a plague: People laid down and died in the middle of the
sidewalk, and those of us still living just walked around the
corpses. *They're sleeping,* we told ourselves; the same line
we feed kids.

The newspapers called it the greenhouse effect. I thought
it was an odd name. It sounded to me as if things were
expected to grow, as if this heat were the preface to a new
creation; what they were describing was a blanket of
deadly gas collecting in the air, through which the sun
could shine, but no heat could escape — a greenhouse.

There seemed to be no way to stop what was happening up there, no way to reverse it. The ball had been set in motion.

What's this? the kid asked me, pointing to a plaque on the wall.

Some award, I said. Nothing much.

What for?

No big deal. Some acting job.

That what you do?

Not right now. Nothing much going on this summer. Most summers.

Cool, he said.

My apartment was filthy. I tried to kid myself that having next to nothing would make life neat — no baggage, no mess. But it's the nature of things to disperse. Dust falls, paint chips scatter, personal objects cascade into corners. My father used to say this was the material consequence of the fall of man. He was a minister; it was his job to come up with things like that. He probably thought he was being funny — which makes him seem pathetic to me now; pathetic and hollow, not much of a man.

I checked the impulse to straighten up, but I left the gate open in front of the fire escape, in case we wanted to go outside for a change of scene. Inside, there was not much to see; it was a one-bedroom apartment in name only, the bedroom being about the size of a coffin. I used it to store my clothes.

I like your place, Christopher said. It's cool.

That made me laugh.

It's old, anyway, I replied.

He went to one of the walls. After looking at it for a minute, he started picking at the paint.

You know what you should do? he said. You should peel away some of this paint. Different layers in different parts.

Why? I asked.

I don't know, he said. It would be different.

I leaned against my desk, the only piece of furniture in the room, apart from an old mattress and a pair of bentwood chairs my sister had bought for me, the one and only time she visited New York. I watched the kid, wondering whether he was going to say something, or whether I would have to. He was still picking at the walls. *This is how it starts*, I thought. *This is how you start to lose it — wondering.*

Or, you could just paint over the whole thing, he said. It's kinda shitty.

He climbed out onto the fire escape and stared out over the railing of the fire escape. He turned his head to the left, looking out over the little courtyard between my building and the one behind it, and the light caught the side of his face in such a way that for a moment he looked very old. It was a startling effect. Then he shifted and leaned his back against the railing, looking in at me, with his arms folded against his chest, his own age again, whatever that was. Twelve. Eight.

You have trees back here, he said.

Yes, I said.

Not everybody does, he replied.

I'm lucky, I said.

I don't believe in luck, he said.

Are you going to come in? I asked.

Sure, he said.

When he came back inside, he pulled a cassette tape out of his pocket and put it in my deck. He rewound it a little ways, then fast-forwarded it, then rewound it again, till he'd found the place he wanted. Then he pushed the play button. Out came a song I had heard a couple of times on the radio. Over and over again it said, Be happy. It didn't make me feel that way. It made me feel resentful. I didn't like being told things. The kid danced around the room.

I love this song, he said.

I watched him for a little while. Sweat was pouring off him now; his T-shirt was soaked. It was very close in my apartment, even with the fan blowing directly on me.

Come here, I said.

He stopped dancing and came towards me, undressing quickly. I pulled back the sheets on the mattress and he flopped onto it and stared up at me smiling while I undressed and lowered myself on top of him. He had a very nice body. I was very attracted to his body. There was no trouble with that. We pressed against each other until we were slick with sweat and then I bent down over him and he lay still for a while, breathing heavily. This went on for quite some time. Then we changed positions. We changed positions again. It wasn't good for me. I was very attracted to him, but I held back. Afterwards, he stroked my hair.

Yes, he said.

I didn't say anything.

Yes, he repeated.

A faint salsa drifted through the window from another apartment off the courtyard. I rested my head next to the kid's, and for a long while we stayed that way, breathing, and listening to the music. It seemed like there was always a point I'd get to, and then I couldn't go any farther. It was always there, this point. Usually I ignored it. Usually, I could pretend that I had gone as far as I wanted to. But today, because of the heat, I couldn't pretend anymore.

The kid sat up and asked me what time it was. I groped

around for my watch among all the sweaty clothes on the
floor.

Five-thirty, I told him.

Better get going, he said.

You can stay, I said.

I can't, he replied.

I'd like you to stay, I said.

He only laughed when I asked him why he couldn't stay.
He said he'd told his girlfriend he'd be home by five. I said I
didn't believe him, and he answered that it wasn't important whether I believed him or not. I said I guessed that was
true, and he said that wasn't important, either.

What is important? I asked.

Doing what you want, he replied.

It isn't so easy, I said.

You do it all the time, he said.

He turned his back to me and started fishing in the tape
deck for his cassette; it was stuck and he had to fiddle with
it for a while. There was a trick to getting it out, but I
wasn't going to tell him what it was.

I guess you want it to stay in there, I said.

When he left, I got up to lock and bolt the door. I stood still
in the middle of the kitchen, trying not to realize that I'd
lost something of real value; squandered it, in fact. I wasn't
sure when it had happened, or if it was the decision of one
moment only; it was that long ago. But I couldn't make any
kind of a leap towards another person now. The gulf of
caution was too wide. On the other side stood an imperceiv-
able unknown.

I tried to fill the empty space with sensation, any kind of
sensation, even if it was painful. I raked at my memory.

Nothing came up; only emptiness. Blank. Bland. Dry.

2

I *TOOK A SHOWER.*

Standing in the tub, letting the water run over me, I heard voices coming through the grate in the ceiling — which was part of a ventilation system connecting several of the apartments on my side of the building.

Two women were arguing. One of them had a shrill, hard voice, and over and over she screamed, *How could you do this to me? How could you do this?* The other woman's voice was low; a moan, almost. I couldn't make out much of what she was saying. It sounded like she was crying, or gagging.

I tried to piece together the entire scene from the bits I overheard. I thought maybe it was the mother and daughter on the third floor, one of the drug and prostitution teams that work in the building. I would be sorry if it was. I liked them a lot, and they were friendly to me, especially the mother. We spoke together when we met in the halls, in a mixture of broken Spanish and English. They had the ugliest dog in the world. They called it Feo, which is Spanish for ugly.

Then again, it might have been the lesbian couple on the first floor. They were always fighting, sometimes violently.

I decided to go to Ceil's for dinner.

It didn't seem so hot out, now that the sun was going

down. There were more people on the street, a lot of them beggars. I tried to ignore them, but in the end I gave money to an old man with no legs, propped up against a storefront. He thanked me as I dropped my change into his cup.

Ceil's was down Ninth a little ways. It had been called Ceil's for as long as I'd lived in the neighborhood, though it had changed owners more than once. One of the bartenders who'd come and gone over the years told me that it was part of the lease to keep the name of the bar. It seemed funny to me that someone would put that in a contract, and it made me wonder who in the world Ceil was, and whether she was still alive. Nobody seemed to know, though, or to care.

Depending on the management at the time, Ceil's was sometimes more of a bar, sometimes more of a restaurant. The changes were never any more dramatic: The food was always pretty much the same. The same people always came. It was fairly dark inside, though never greasy or dingy. None of the owners ever thought of changing the carpet, a worn dirty green, the color of old Astroturf.

An old friend of mine, Stu Vivitski, was sitting at a table with a girl when I arrived. They had just ordered, but Vivitski waved me over to join them, anyway. I didn't want to at first, but then I thought, what the hell. The waitress, a big-boned girl with unnatural red hair, took my order, and after shouting it into the kitchen and bringing me a beer, she stood at the bar fraternizing with the bartender and one or two of the drinking customers, leaning with her hip against the counter.

Vivitski and I had been at acting school together. He was the only person I still saw from those days, largely because he lived in the neighborhood. I didn't like him all that much. He was fairly stupid. He reminded me of a big dog, all slobbery and ready to hump your leg if it wasn't moving. He always went out with strange, pale girls, who hardly ever talked when they came out with us, hardly ate. They just smiled and stared at the space between the salt and pepper shakers, which could be either unnerving or irritating, depending on your mood.

This new girl was a lot prettier than some of the others, with long brown hair held back with a band. But she was very thin, and when she laughed, she sort of slid her mouth to one side, as if it wasn't quite appropriate. Her name was Pam. I kept calling her Patty, by mistake, until Vivitski finally corrected me. I saw how sad the girl looked, and I apologized to her. She said it wasn't that. I had no idea what she meant.

How 'bout this heat? Vivitski asked.

How about it, I replied.

Rough, Vivitski said.

The food came, and we ordered another round of drinks. I was very thirsty, which is one of the consequences of summer that I always forget. After she brought us our drinks, the waitress took a long look at Vivitski and said,

You're famous, aren't you?

Well, Vivitski said.

No, some of the guys at the bar said you were in a movie, she explained. One of them saw you on TV.

Could be, Vivitski said.

Was it you? the waitress asked.

I don't know, Vivitski replied. What was the movie?

I don't know, the waitress said.

Someone at another table waved to her.

I have to work this whole place by myself, she said as she walked away from us.

We ate. Vivitski asked me how things were and I said

they were not great. I'd had a falling out with my agent. It was the third time in two months.

Comedy comes in threes, Vivitski said.

Yeah, I agreed.

What's that mean? Pam asked.

Vivitski ignored her.

You dump him? he asked me.

What do you mean? Pam repeated.

No, I said.

He dump you? Vivitski asked.

Pam got a stricken look on her face, and I started to feel very uncomfortable in my chair. I had a hard time with Vivitski ignoring her. I told her how in comedies there are three parts to a joke. There's the setup — say, the first time somebody slips on a banana peel; that's funny enough in itself. The second time someone slips there's a build, and the audience has a sense of something larger going on. The third time is the payoff, and gets the big laugh because the audience is lifted completely out of the world of the possible and into another place altogether. They're in on the joke, part of the process of it. You can see the same sort of thing in some of those farmer's daughter jokes; three guys, each one dumber than the next, and the last guy is the butt of the whole thing.

Pam nodded.

It's an old thing, I explained.

Yeah, she said.

Vivitski put his arm around her.

Isn't she beautiful? he said.

He kissed her on the cheek.

She's so beautiful, he said.

The waitress came back over. The guy at the bar had told her the name of the movie he thought he'd seen Vivitski in, and Vivitski said that was the one, and the waitress turned around and shouted,

Hey, Jay, it *is* him!

Jay, sitting on a bar stool, swiveled around. He had big fuzzy patches of hair on each side of his head and nothing in the middle. He smiled. The other people at the bar turned to look in our direction.

Hey, how'd you do that part climbing up the side of the building? the man named Jay asked.

I can't tell you, Vivitski said. I signed a contract that said I wouldn't give away trade secrets.

That's a line, I whispered to Pam.

She smiled.

Well, it was a great picture, Jay said.

Thanks, Vivitski said.

Jay sent a round of drinks to our table. We toasted him and he raised his glass to us, and some of the other people at the bar said, Cheers. Vivitski ordered another round and sent a drink to Jay.

You're famous too, a woman at the bar said to me.

No, I said. No, I'm not.

Yes you are, she insisted, I've seen you.

No, really, I said. I'm not.

I know I've seen you, she said.

Well, I said.

Maybe she has, Vivitski argued.

I'd be surprised, I said.

So be surprised, he said.

I was starting to get drunk.

You're coming with us, Vivitski said.

Where? I asked.

Party, he said.

No, I said. No party. I hate parties.

No, you're coming with us, Vivitski argued.

He threw a heavy arm around my shoulder and squeezed me close to him, and I was overpowered by the smell of his sweat and cologne.

Pam wants you to come, he said. She likes you.

Please come, Pam said.

I looked at her. There was desperation in her face, and I thought, while we might have nothing else in common, there was no doubt we had the same feeling about people. A sudden urge to insult her came over me — I knew I could, and knowing it made me feel guilty. I agreed to go.

Vivitski paid the tab. He didn't make a show of it; he just laid a bill on the table, leaving the waitress a big tip, and said, Let's go.

We went outside. The air was heavy, curling around people, lampposts, garbage cans, and in the glare of the streetlights it showed up white. There was a fruity odor, too; the smell of rotting food. Pam covered her nose. Vivitski stepped out in the street to hail a cab.

Not walking in this shit, he muttered.

It took a long time for a cab to come, and while we waited we were treated to a lot of commotion on the street. Troops of kids, holding their blaring music boxes aloft, shook and rattled down the street, throwing bottles and kicking cans. A man came along, dogged by a woman who was shouting at him, *And now I'm knocked up and you're gonna hit me, you bastard, now I'm knocked up and you're gonna hit me?* Another man walked right up to a wall behind us and pulled open his pants and pissed. The urine smell permeated everything. A woman, sitting on the stoop nearby with her children, screamed at him to stop exposing himself to her kids.

Pam stepped out into the street and stood next to Vivitski. I stayed where I was, caught between trying to bear it all and trying to ignore it.

Finally, a cab stopped at the corner and let out a heavy-set guy wearing only a T-shirt and shorts that exposed his pale, veiny legs. I thought he must be feeling the heat pretty badly, to be wearing shorts; his legs had probably never seen the sun. He reminded me of an uncle of mine, also a heavyset man, who was so ashamed of the way his legs looked that he would never let anyone see them. Not even in the height of summer; not even to go swimming. I remember my father making fun of him.

The cab was air-conditioned. Vivitski gave the driver the address and we rolled down Ninth Avenue; the burning heat was not our problem anymore.

Vivitski talked about his upcoming job. I talked about the fight I'd had with my agent. Pam sat between us, looking neither right nor left. Neither of us thought to include her in our conversation. We were comfortable ignoring her, and she seemed comfortable that way.

We got out at Tenth Street and Fourth. I said I'd pay for the ride, and after a little argument, Vivitski let me. We crossed the street. On the far corner a woman with her two kids leaned against a brick wall; the kids were asleep, but the mother was not. She held out her hand to us as we walked by, and in the light of the streetlamp we could see how thin she was; her hair was pulled back from her face and we could see her bones. Her eyes were quite round and protruding. She had a sore just above her lip. In front of her was a styrofoam cup and a cardboard sign saying they were homeless, etc. I didn't know whether or not to believe it. Some mothers were using their kids now for sympathy, just to get money for a fix; some mothers were selling their kids

sexually. I threw my change from the cab into her cup. I
hated the idea of her using her kids as an excuse, if that's
what she was doing. She just stared right past me. There
was so much in that vacancy; my self-righteousness felt
very small in comparison.

Vivitski threw some change into her cup, too.

We went down Tenth, stopping halfway down the block
at a building with a yellow bulb in the lamp over its door.
We went up the steps, and Vivitski rang the bell. When the
door buzzed, we pushed into an ugly hallway with bright
fluorescent lights, and followed it back towards the party
sounds. The apartment door was wide open. Already there
was a huge crowd inside. I thought almost immediately that
the best thing would be to turn around and go.

The place was too bright. It had white walls and
bleached-out floors. There were some line drawings on the
wall, nothing too colorful. Somewhere, a stereo was blasting. It occurred to me that I'd forgotten to ask Vivitski
whose party it was, and why we were going; but it was too
late now. He pressed through the foyer and Pam and I
followed right behind, a little anxious about the space he
opened closing before we got through. All around me, I
glimpsed faces; some turning to stare; some turning to say
hello; some engrossed in conversation, ignoring us. I caught
a few glances of interest and shifted to stare at the small of
Pam's tight back. She seemed to be hanging on to Vivitski's
arm with great strength. The whole passage was disorient-
ing. Nothing seemed to be particularly connected; it was a
jumble of sounds and flesh and sensations.

We got to the kitchen just in time to find the host — a
short, dark man, with catlike features — on his way to the
living room carrying a huge bottle of champagne. He was
very happy to see Vivitski and stood on tiptoe to kiss him

on the cheek. He greeted Pam nicely, and gave me a warm once-over; then he turned his back on us to talk to Vivitski. It made me laugh. Vivitski always made friends with homosexual men he never intended to sleep with. He didn't mind the attention, and they didn't mind giving it to him. It was a kind of barter.

From the kitchen someone handed me a glass spilling over with champagne, and I had to drink fast to keep the bubbles from covering my hands. It was cool and tangy going down, the first really refreshing sensation I'd experienced all day — all summer, it seemed. I drained my glass, probably too quickly, and thrust it in the direction of the freckle-faced young man standing across from me holding a half-empty bottle.

What's the occasion? I shouted to him, above the music and the talking. What are we celebrating?

I don't know, he shouted back to me. I only live here!

Thanks, I said to him, when he finished pouring me a new glass. Do you really?

What?

Live here?

No, he shouted. I'm just a friend of a friend.

Of a friend of a friend? I added.

Exactly, he agreed.

He poured himself another glass.

I guess we're all strangers here then, I said.

I had intended it as a joke, but he just looked at me, kind of startled, and nodded.

Right, he said.

A group of eight or ten people surged all together through the crowded hall just then, and seeing them behind me, my conversation partner smiled, very relieved. He started towards them, passing the champagne bottle to me:

I moved out of his way, backing up and turning to face the new group. They all looked happy and graceful and sporty, and as they squeezed around the freckle-faced young man, I suddenly found myself face-to-face with someone I hadn't seen in a long time.

Hello, old man, she said.

Hey, I said.

She was very pretty and very tan. Her hair was short, which was not how I remembered it. She looked very lithe with it short; nimble, ready to spring, like something from a darker continent.

Friend of the bride or friend of the groom? I asked her.

Friend of the groom, she said.

She nodded to Freckle-Face, who was now talking with a tall, blond man: Paul.

That one used to be with Paul, she said.

I watched them talk. They looked very easy with each other.

They must have ended on good terms, I said.

Some people do, Kate replied.

Lucky them, I said.

Lucky them, she agreed.

She looked at the bottle in my hands.

Could I have some? she asked. I'm parched.

There's only my glass, I said — unable to think of anything else to say.

I don't care, she said.

I poured what was left in the bottle. There wasn't much; it only filled the glass about two-thirds of the way. I set the empty bottle on the floor and handed the glass to Kate.

I'm sorry, I said.

I'll bet there's more, she said.

You're right, I said. You're probably right.

Not always, she said.

I nodded. I felt very awkward standing there. The last time I'd seen her I told a lie, thinking I was doing her a favor. I told her I had to leave town to see an aunt somewhere, who was dying. I never returned any of her telephone calls after I was supposed to have come back. She knew I was lying. She'd seen me invent dying relatives before, to get out of situations. She'd heard me describe in detail the deathbed scenes of people who were still living.

I should go, I said now. I have to go.

I squeezed through the crowd without waiting for her to say anything. I didn't even think of saying good-bye to Vivitski or to Pam. I could always tell them I'd gotten lost in the press — which brought to mind something I'd heard a long time ago: *We're about truth! You're not about truth!*

I felt a little bad for Pam as I walked out, but she wasn't my problem. I wouldn't let her be my problem.

It was good to be outside again, standing on the stone steps. I liked the darkness and the solitude. The weather had taken a turn; a wind was rising. I figured it would probably rain soon, so I'd better get going, but I stayed on the steps for a minute longer and lit a cigarette. On a radio somewhere, someone was crooning, *I want you want you baby want you bad.* Probably just a metaphor. I threw the match off the side of the steps, and watched the flame go out before it hit the ground. Kate came out behind me.

You're not getting away like that, she said.

I jumped.

Jesus Christ, I said, turning around. You scared me.

Poor you, Kate said.

I went down the steps to the sidewalk. I wanted to keep
some distance between us.

Where do you think you're going? she asked.

Home, I said.

Take me with you, she said.

I can't. I can't do that.

Let's go for a drink.

No, I said. No.

You won't come inside? she asked.

No, I said. Just no.

Tell me why you lied, then, she said. That's all.

I pitched my cigarette butt onto the tar and ground it
with my toe.

I didn't want to see you, I told her.

I wish you'd said so, she said.

Right, I said. Right.

Kate lit a cigarette and threw the match away. I looked
her in the eyes. She had great eyes, moist and dark. They
didn't go well with the rest of her face, but I liked them all
the more for that.

We had a death in my family, she said to me. A real one.

Yes?

My father, she said. You would have liked it. He died at
home.

Not me, I said. I want to be far away when my old man
goes. I want to be on the moon.

I know, Kate said. I know.

She was pretty, standing underneath the porch light with
the smoke billowing around her. The yellow light made her
look coppery-colored. She smiled at me. I stood on the
sidewalk, just looking at her. It started to rain.

Better come in, Kate said.

I shook my head.

You'll get wet, she said.

I nodded.

My choice, I said.

What's the deal? she asked.

There's no deal, I replied.

What's the problem? she asked.

There's no problem, I said.

Then come in.

I shook my head again.

I hate you, I said.

She shrugged.

Not my problem, she said.

Something rotten gathered inside my chest; gathered, but didn't break. The rain started to come down in earnest. Bullets. Pellets. Hard.

We're about truth, I said.

What?

We're about truth, I repeated.

She laughed, and reached out her hand to me.

Stupid, she said. *So* stupid.

The rain made a slapping sound on the pavement. I almost took the hand she offered. But at the last minute I got hold of myself and turned around and started up the street. The rain soaked me to the skin. I didn't care — it would remind me not to look back. If I looked back I'd dissolve.

3

THE RAIN STOPPED SHORT of turning into a full-fledged storm. There was no thunder or lightning, only a steady, soaking barrage of water. When I got home, I peeled out of my wet clothes, hung them in the bathroom, dried off, and put on a pair of jogging shorts. The rain had soaked through the cigarettes in my shirt pocket. I found a half-smoked one in the ashtray, lit it, and stared out the window at the rain.

I'd gone out looking for someone to tell me I was all right. Vivitski's girl might have, but she was too easy. Kate would have, but it would have meant giving up all my strength; and the only strength I had was in resistance.

I sat at the window for an hour, watching the downpour, turning things over. It was still raining when I went to bed, but it didn't do anything to take away the heat.

I'd met her in a drugstore; she was buying Band-Aids, I was buying cigarettes. I noticed she was limping and asked if I could help. She told me she'd stubbed her toe coming down the stairs of her apartment and now it was bleeding.

The toe, she said, not the apartment.

We sat on the sidewalk in front of the drugstore and I bandaged her up, and afterwards she kissed me on the nose and called me old man. I liked that. Then we hobbled down the street to a divey little bar off Union Square, with a tin ceiling and seventy-five-cent hamburgers. Cheap was the operative word for us, then.

I'd been in the city for about five months, and she was the first openly nice person I'd met. She told me she was working for a man named Roth, who was round and shiny like a wax pear and designed interiors for very ritzy people, and if I needed the cash and could spare the time, she knew he'd like help a few hours every other day or so, to sort things and file things, and maybe clean some. I was grateful. The pay filled out what I'd saved before coming to New York, which wasn't enough. She didn't mention that Roth had wandering hands; it wasn't a problem for her, particularly. Being around this vivacious, pretty girl was terrific. We went out a lot — not to particularly grand places, but grand enough. She figured me pretty quickly, and maybe she was a little disappointed, maybe relieved. Anyway, we had a lot of fun together.

About four months after I was hired on at Roth's, though, Kate was sacked. She kept making helpful suggestions, and Roth ended up telling her she was insubordinate. She was crushed. I don't think she had any idea. It ended up being all right for me, because I got her job along with mine and a raise in salary. But I didn't see her again for a long time. She took off after Paul, who was dancing in Europe at the time; that was how I first heard about him. Every blue moon over the next couple of years, Kate would send me a postcard of some statue she'd fallen in love with, and she'd always scrawl on the back that it reminded her of me. I thought that was pretty funny.

When she came back, I was out of acting school, and doing something down in the East Village: Political theatre — a

lot of stamping around with signs and helmets, singing
songs like Down With Capitalism. One choice number had
a girl, representing Cuba, who took off her clothes and
spread her legs to take Soviet missiles. I told Kate all about
it, the night we met again over drinks.

When can I come? she asked.

You don't want to, I said.

Yes I do, she said. I want to see you. I like a light evening
in the theatre.

There aren't a lot of lights, I told her. It's poor theatre.
It's more dark than light.

I like a dim evening in the theatre, she said.

She coaxed a little more, and finally I said she could
come. The next night would be good for her, she said, and
since the tickets weren't anything like scarce, I told her the
next night would probably be fine.

Good, she said. Now I'll see you.

I mentioned, too, that there was going to be a party after
the performance, some of the cast getting together, and I
asked her if she would like to go with me.

I'd be delighted, she said.

Really? I asked.

Charmed, she said.

That's a funny word, I said.

Is it?

It's very formal.

I don't want to be formal, she said.

I watched her light a cigarette and blow the smoke up
into the light, where it circled and clung. She was, in fact, a
very casual person. All her moves were fluid, she was easy
to talk to. In comparison, I felt like some old sort of crab, all
hard-shelled limbs, snapping.

How about if I order another round of drinks? I asked.

Can we afford it?

Probably not.

All right then, she said. Let's have one more round.

I'm glad you're back, I said, surprised at myself.

Me too, old man, she said. It was terrible over there, terrible.

She looked sad just then, puffing on her cigarette. I wondered what had happened. For an instant her pupils went wide and dark, and out of them poured something beautiful and unapproachable. It was a look of someone who had seen the worst — and lived, which was just as bad.

Are you going to make it? I asked.

What? Yes. I'll get by.

Did you and what's-his-name, Paul, fall out?

She laughed, and stubbed out her smoke.

What's-his-name-Paul and I have an understanding, she said. We'll never fall out.

Good, I said. That's good.

I ordered another round from the waitress when she went by, and we drank it quickly. Kate talked about the pictures she'd been taking while she was away, and how she hoped to sell them now. She was pretty sure she could; a lot of people had told her they were good. I wished her the best. She got up to go shortly afterwards, saying she had to meet somebody. She laid some money on the table, not enough to cover her share, but at least she didn't leave me to pay the whole tab. I was glad of that. I ordered another couple of beers for myself and sat thinking how really happy I was that she was back.

The next night she came to the show, and it went well enough; it was Halloween, though, and it seemed to me that there were more costumes in the audience than on the

stage — better ones, too. Afterwards, Kate and I went out for a couple of beers and had a good laugh together about the whole thing. Then the bar got crowded, so we hopped a cab and went farther downtown and farther east than I had ever gone, beyond Alphabet City, to the address of the party — which is a place I'm sure no longer exists. It has to have dropped into hell by now, because it was teetering pretty far over the edge back then. It was a scary place. Clinton and Stanton streets; I only remember the names because they sounded like lost explorers.

The host of the party was standing in the front room greeting people when we came in. He was dressed all in green, with green makeup on, and he had a parrot on his shoulder that was leaving a white trail of droppings down his back.

Very attractive, I said, when I saw him.

He kissed me full on the lips, tongue lashing down my throat, the parrot squawking. Then he moved to do the same thing to Kate, but she backed away. He didn't seem to mind; he stuffed his hand in his shirt pocket, pulled out some capsules, and offered them to us.

What are they? I asked him.

I dunno, he said, and smiled, showing a gap between his teeth.

No thanks, I said.

None for me, Kate said. I'm driving.

Suit yaselves, he replied.

He shoved them back in his pocket, except for one, which he tried to feed the parrot. The bird was not amused. Kate and I pushed into the smoke-filled blackness where something like music trembled violently in the air.

I love your friends, Kate commented.

A few people were dancing in an area lit a little more brightly, but most everyone was sitting in groups of two or three, talking. Looking around, I noticed that everyone else at the party was in costume. It dawned on me that I had forgotten to put that together with the idea of going to a party on Halloween. It looked as if Kate and I had come dressed up as people from New Rochelle.

Do you wanna dance? I asked her.

Not yet, Kate said. Let's have a drink.

I set down the bag I was carrying and pulled out a couple of cans from the six-pack we had brought. Kate started to put her purse on the floor, then changed her mind.

Do you think if I put this down someone will steal it? she asked me.

I don't know, I said.

I hope so, she said, putting it down next to her chair. I hate this purse.

I laughed, and cracked open a can for her and a can for me. We sat very close to each other on a bench, watching people dance. She was wearing a nice perfume, I noticed. The music was very loud; even sitting close we almost had to shout.

What kind of acting do you want to do? Kate asked me. When you're grown.

I want to sit in a chair and smoke cigarettes and be bitter, I told her. I want to imitate life.

That's dull, she replied. Wouldn't you rather invent it?

You mean the old girl has a few tricks left?

I bet there are a few surprises, she said.

Maybe, I said.

Will anyone see you in this play? she asked.

I'll be lucky if I don't get arrested doing it, I said.

Something will turn up, Kate said.

Plague, I said. Probably.

We drank without saying anything for a couple of minutes, and then I lit a couple of cigarettes and offered her one.

What do you want to do? I asked.

She reflected a minute.

This, she said. I wish I had a camera with me right now. I would like to catch this.

We should have come as tourists, I said.

A short fat man in a dark sweater and white clown makeup spotted me; the director of the show. He came over and asked me if I wanted to dance. I looked at Kate and gestured and demurred. Kate gestured that it was all right with her. I tried to signal her telepathically that I hoped she developed something very uncomfortable on her skin, then I followed the director up to the middle of the floor. I jumped around a little as he gyrated and thrust his hips at me and made strange faces, which I supposed were meant to signify attraction. I didn't want to laugh at him, so I kept looking at Kate looking at us over the rest of the room.

The next dance was a slow one, and before I could get away Lauren had pulled me close and wrapped his arms around me and laid his cheek against mine, leaving what I was afraid would be a little slick of sweat and white pancake on my face. He held me very close and ground his pelvis into mine and whispered wetly in my ear how he thought I was hot, and how he wanted to make love to me. I told him I thought that was nice of him, and that if circumstances were different I probably would; but unfortunately for both of us the thing was that I was straight, and so men didn't really turn me on at all. He responded by saying he had heard that I was not straight; to which I said no, I was.

Then he said he was sure I was not straight, and again I said no. Finally he said there was someone in the cast who told him I was not straight; and still I said no. After a couple more turns, he started feeding me a line about genital-role boundaries and how they were symptomatic of the depths to which the unnatural morality of evil capitalism had penetrated, and that if I made it with him it was the moral equivalent of divesting in South Africa or feeding the children of Bophal. I told him I preferred giving to UNICEF.

Meanwhile, each time Lauren and I turned in our little circuit I saw Kate sitting there, cigarette in hand, a kind of Virgin Mary smile on her face, watching, ringed with a halo of smoke and light. Then we would turn again, and she would vanish from my line of sight; we'd turn again, and she'd be back. I thought, seeing her so still, so present, she was hands down the most interesting person in the room. She was filled with a look of potential, a look of private annunciation, which lit her up from within. I was almost jealous.

After I finally got away from Lauren, I went back to Kate and stood drinking my beer. I was very hot and uncomfortable. I was glad when somebody finally turned down the music.

I loved your face, Kate said. When you were dancing.

He stank, I said. He was very drunk and he stank of it.

I could tell what you were thinking.

I thought I was opaque.

I could tell, Kate said.

How? I asked.

Later. When we know each other more.

I want to know now, I said.

Later, she said. Here comes your friend.

I looked where she nodded; Lauren was coming back through the crowd like a great shark. He had Mike with him, one of the cast, and Mike had a grim, embarrassed expression on his face. He wouldn't look me in the eye. I wondered if Lauren was hurting his arm where he grabbed it.

Mike says you and he were together last week, Lauren said.

Does he? I said.

That makes you a liar, Lauren said. That makes you a liar to me.

My face started getting hot as he stared. I couldn't think of anything to say.

Yes, well, I finally said. I'm a liar.

I thought Lauren might do something hysterical. He was quite drunk. But he just weaved a little bit, unsteady on his feet; his eyes went small and bestial.

You're a pig, he said to me.

I nodded.

Yes, I said. I am a pig.

I don't want you around, he said.

All right, I said, nodding again. I thought by being calm and letting him have his say, he would quiet down, but my answers only seemed to make him angrier. He raised the pitch of his voice, speaking more emphatically, and tried to make himself taller by standing on his toes.

I mean I don't want you in the company, he said. I don't want you in the piece.

Fine, I replied. If that's what you want.

We're about truth, he said.

It's not like you're paying me, I reminded him. Not like it's going to break me.

You're a liar, he insisted.

Come on, Mike said.

Behind me, Kate lit up a cigarette. Lauren glanced away from me and looked her over. I watched his face go slack, and then he squared back on me.

Pretty beard, he said.

My arm went back. Kate saw it and stood up. She got in between us, and I had no choice but to let my arm drop back down to my side.

You're tough, aren't you? Lauren said to me. A real tough guy.

Come on, Kate said. Come on, let's go.

You think you're tough, Lauren said. You don't know from what you are.

Come on, Kate said.

Do what she says, Lauren said. Your girlfriend.

He wants you to hit him, Kate said to me. It would make him feel good.

What do you know? Lauren asked.

I bet I know, Kate said.

I bet you do, Lauren replied.

I leaned over and picked up the bag with the rest of our beer in it. Kate had a funny smile on her face, as though it were not at all serious, just a big joke; she started walking and I followed her.

Just remember you're fired, Lauren called after me.

I remember, I answered.

We're about truth! he repeated, shouting.

We snaked past the host of the party, who was trying to get his parrot to drink out of a bottle of vodka, but the bird kept rearing back and beating its wings and squawking. A girl dressed in tinfoil was watching the whole process. Suddenly, she leaned over and threw up on the floor.

We went outside. I was mad and Kate could see it. But

she dove right in. She wasn't afraid. That was interesting. Some people might have turned away, or made a joke; taken cover in some way.

What's a beard? she asked me.

A disguise, I said. A mask.

Is that what I am?

No.

Not even partly?

We walked down the street a ways in silence.

No, I said.

Maybe to fool yourself? Even partly?

Maybe partly, I said.

Good, she said. I'm glad. If you'd said no you would have been fooling yourself. We're about truth.

She laughed.

I didn't like him, I said. That's all it was.

Because he wanted to be with you, Kate said.

Because he was out of control, I said. I don't like people out of control.

You might have told him the truth, Kate said.

Please, I said.

You should be flattered, she said.

Please, I repeated.

When someone likes you, she said, you should be flattered.

We could have gotten mugged walking down that street. There were a lot of dangerous-looking people standing in doorways, or tooling up and down, broken glass crunching under their boots. They looked us over as we passed. Now close, now far, there was a burst of laughter, or a sharp boom like gunshot — probably just a truck passing over a metal plate in the middle of the street. I was glad when we finally walked north far enough to find a cab. We took it up to Fourteenth Street, which was near Kate's apartment, and all we could afford between us.

I'd invite you to come up with me, Kate said when we got out. But I'm sure Paul's asleep.

You've been together a long time, I said.

Oh dear, she said. Oh no.

She started laughing. We walked over and sat on one of the benches in the park, which were occupied mainly by drunks and junkies and sleeping pigeons.

I didn't mean that I was interested, I said. I didn't mean it to sound like that.

He's my brother, Kate said.

Oh, I said. I thought —

Obviously, she said, leaning back on the park bench and pulling a cigarette out of her coat pocket. I fumbled for a match. When I lit her cigarette she had to brush her hair back; it was very long then, and dyed red. She blew the smoke out quickly, and it dispersed almost immediately. The night was very cool and clear. There was a small, bright blue moon. I opened a beer for her and one for me.

Paul would be nice to be with, she said. Everyone says.

Everyone?

He has a lot of friends. He's lovely. Blond. Tall. I wish he were my husband, sometimes.

You might have strange-looking children, I said.

No, she said. We wouldn't have any.

She tapped her belly.

All fucked up, she said.

I wasn't sure whether to ask or change the subject, so I let the moment hang. She finished her cigarette, then told me that she'd almost been a miscarriage, and her mother had taken a pill that was quite common in those days to prevent such a thing from happening. Kate ended up being born, all

right, but because of the pill she was terribly thwarted on
the reproductive side of things. For all intents and purposes
she was barren.

Sins of the mothers, she concluded.

That's a strong word, I said.

It would have been better not to tamper, Kate said. You
can't stop anything from dying.

Besides, she continued, my mother was a terrible woman.
She left when Paul and I were tots. Ran off with a friend of
my father's, a painter. She used to model for him. My
father brought home all sorts of women to take her place,
after. I lit a lot of candles for my father.

You're a Catholic? I asked.

She nodded.

You? she asked.

No, I said.

I lit candles for my mother, too, she said. Wherever she
was. Wherever she is.

Do you believe in that? I asked her. God?

Yes, she said.

A group of teenage girls trooped by, laughing, wearing
witch costumes: black capes, pointed hats. One of them
had a broom. We watched them; they were having a good
time, out enjoying themselves.

People work so hard at being good, I said. And they get
nothing back. They get cancer. Their dogs die. I don't believe in it. God.

Is that what it's supposed to be about? Getting things
back?

It's not about losing things, is it? I asked. Things taken
away from you?

I tossed my cigarette as far as it would go and lit another

one. It was getting late, past midnight. A couple of werewolves stumbled by, and a vampire; a few ghosts. There were more and more cabs, filled with people in costumes, coming home from parties.

My father's a minister, I said.

Oh my, Kate said.

I usually say he teaches, I said. Or that he's dead.

Why?

It's embarrassing. You're supposed to be good.

Aren't you good?

No.

Neither am I. I'm awful.

Me too.

Good.

Let's have another beer, why don't we?

Yes, let's.

I opened up the last two beer cans from our six-pack. Kate lit another cigarette, and moved a little closer to me. She shivered.

That's why I need God, she said. I have to believe someone loves me, bad as I am.

I thought God punished bad people, I said.

Priests punish, Kate said. God doesn't hold what I've done against me.

It's all balls, I said. Junk.

It still works, she replied.

I didn't say anything for a minute or two.

I was out with my father once, I said, finally. He started in about family life. He started in about women and marriage, and how holy it all was. I felt so rotten, listening to him. It was obvious he hated my mother and she hated him. They were only staying together for some sort of show, for this act they put on Sunday after Sunday. I didn't say anything to him, though. I let him go on. I played the same trick he and everybody else played week after week.

It must be hard to be a minister, Kate said.

He's up in the clouds, I said. Up there talking face-to-face with God, like it's some old uncle who drops by on the weekends.

That's rich, Kate said.

The only time I ever saw the face of God, I said, was when I told my sister I didn't believe in God — and she turned around and said she didn't, either. We laughed till it hurt. That was the face of God.

Your mother?

She bought it, or said she did.

Where's your sister now?

In Wisconsin, I said. With a family of her own. Which she brings to church.

Right, Kate said.

She looked up at the moon.

Is that why you're queer? she asked.

What? I said.

She flicked her cigarette butt onto the pavement like a hoodlum, expertly. She turned to me. That look came into her eyes again, the one I'd seen in the bar the night before.

The impulse to adore, she said, runs so very deep.

We started going out more and more after that night; Kate called it hunting. She liked to watch me. At first I was self-conscious, aware of her when I talked to someone; but I got used to her being there, and sometimes it felt wrong when she wasn't. I wouldn't say that I ever picked up somebody just because she was watching, and I don't think she ever did because I was: It wasn't sporting unless the attraction was genuine. But to know that someone was watching added something to the game.

Sometimes Paul joined us, which wasn't much fun. He'd turn most heads right away, and right away he'd hook a young, fresh type. There wasn't much sport in the way Paul worked; it seemed almost mean. Kate said it was because he was in a cut-short profession, a career where people's bodies just collapsed in pain, right at the time when most other people are hitting their stride.

There were ugly incidents between Kate and me, fits and starts of jealousy; but in the main, we kept it pretty light. When I started to go out of town a lot for work, and she went off somewhere to take pictures, it might be strange when we met again, but sooner or later we'd laugh it off.

One afternoon we got high. I'd been out of work for a long time and was starting to get weird about it, and a friend of mine gave me something, saying, *This'll cure you.* I shared it with Kate because she was having headaches — the effect of winter, she said, too much winter. The thing we took was called Ecstasy.

At first it was cozy and warm and we sat in front of the fireplace watching the flames jump through each other, making shapes and patterns. I don't even know when it got to be more than that, just that in the middle of everything I was suddenly aware of telling her how beautiful I thought she was — and really seeing it, too — and then I was kissing her. Suddenly we were sweating and half-naked, and I was touching her breasts, which I'd never thought about before. I said I loved her, and then we were naked and she was fitting me inside herself with her finger and I wasn't embarrassed or ashamed. We were making love, on the floor of the loft she shared with Paul, and I was hard inside her; and it was strange, not the strange of awful, but

the strange of never thinking this would happen to me. I
lost control. I came so long and hard, and so did she. Then
we rolled apart and smoked cigarettes and talked about all
sorts of things — my mother, my father, her father, her
brother — things we'd told no other living being. And then
we made love again, and again; it wasn't until the middle of
the last time that this cold clench hit me deep down inside
my stomach and in my heart, and I knew the drug was
wearing off, and I hadn't meant half the things I'd said to
her; but I had a sneaking suspicion from the way she felt all
relaxed and wide underneath me that she had meant what
she said, and what was worse, had also really believed me,
and I couldn't finish. I got soft inside her, and finally I
pulled out. We smoked a few more cigarettes and a couple
of joints, and after a while Kate fell asleep. I stayed awake
trying to think of an honest way out of the situation, but
nothing came to me; the next day when we woke up I lied
and told her I was going to visit a sick aunt.

I never returned her calls after that. She went away to
New Mexico to stay with some artists in the desert. A few
weeks later, I got a film job out of town. I was glad to be
gone.

When I came back, it was summer.

4

IN THE MIDDLE OF THE NIGHT, after the rain died down, some desperate addict buzzed my apartment from downstairs. They do that sometimes, when they aren't sure which bell to ring; they'll ring every buzzer till someone lets them in, and then try every apartment until they get one of the dealers in the building. There was a time when I felt sorry for them and let them in. Now I was tired of it. I hardly ever got up even to tell them they had the wrong bell.

This one was bad off. He — or she — kept pressing against my bell long and hard. I couldn't stand it after a while, and I got out of bed and went into the kitchen to ring him in.

It turned out to be more than one. I could hear them stumbling through the hallway downstairs, talking in low voices, slurring their words, looking for the right apartment. I felt a powerful resentment rise up against them for waking me up, and I stood by my door waiting for them to knock, so I could tell them to go to hell.

It didn't take long for them to get to my door.

Wrong goddamn apartment, I said.

In the hall, there was a quick, muffled argument. It sounded like there were three or four people, and at least two of them were angry with the person who was leading them. I didn't like the idea of a crowd of people outside my door and I wished they'd move on soon. I gave them the apartment number of one of the dealers in the building, and said that was the place they wanted. One of the voices then spoke to me, a woman's voice.

What? she asked.

I repeated the apartment number, and they muttered among themselves a little more.

That's the one you want, I repeated.

Are you sure? the woman's voice asked.

Positive, I replied.

Bag of shit, she said.

Excuse me? I said.

Bag of shit, she repeated. Presumptuous bag of shit.

Hey, hey, another voice beyond the door soothed.

Well, how the hell does he know what I want? she asked. How the hell does he know?

She banged on my door with a heavy object.

Hey, piece of shit, she said. Open up.

Maybe it *is* the wrong apartment, the soothing voice said.

It's the apartment, the woman said. I know it is. I've been in this apartment.

I don't think so, I said through the door.

I don't think so, the woman mocked. What do you wanna bet?

I don't want to bet anything, I said. I want you to go away or I'll call the police.

I'll bet you, the woman said. If I'm right, you give me three wishes.

She then described the inside of my apartment, more or less accurately.

Who are you? I asked, putting my eye up to the peephole and pressing the button that opened it. But I couldn't see anything; someone on the other side had a hand — or something — pressed against the lens on that side.

First wish, the woman said, is to let us in.

I know you, I said. I have to know you.

Maybe, the woman said. But maybe you don't.

There was a loud popping sound right outside the door, like a paper bag filled with air bursting. Startled, I backed away from the door a little, then felt something wet around my feet; looking down, I saw some kind of clear, yellowish liquid seeping in under the crack of the door.

Time's up, the woman said. We've made our offering, now let us in, old man.

Shit, I whispered. Oh shit.

I slid the bolt and fiddled with the locks.

Kate was kneeling by the door, pouring champagne over the sill. As the door swung open, she stopped what she was doing and looked up at me.

Second wish, she said, is for some glasses for my friends and me. And you, too. It's a little warm, but there's lots. Lots in the car.

Come on in, I said.

She turned to Paul and another man, who were both standing behind her and said, First wish wasn't so hard.

Paul helped Kate to her feet, and they crossed the threshold, stepping widely to avoid the puddle of champagne spreading over the kitchen floor. The third guy followed them, nodding to me and smiling uncomfortably. He was short and nervous-looking, with light brown curly hair sticking to his head.

This is Robb, Kate said, pointing to him.

We would have shaken hands, except that he was carrying two more bottles of champagne. He held them up and grinned. I nodded, and closed the door behind them and ducked into the bathroom to get a sponge to clean up the wine on the floor.

Glasses are over the sink, I said.

I know, Kate said. I've been here before.

Nice place, Robb said.

He had a nice face, sweet and harmless; a doll's face.

Have a seat, I told him.

If you can find one, Kate said. It's a game. You have to dash for a chair, or you're out.

At least out of luck, Paul said, lying down on my mattress.

Clean sheets, he observed.

He was expecting us, Kate said.

No I wasn't, I said to Kate.

Having cleaned up the floor as best I could, I rinsed the sponge in the kitchen sink, and washed my hands.

Well, we're here now, Kate rejoined.

She brought four glasses into the other room and sat on the edge of the bed to pour. Paul sat up. I followed her, taking one of the bentwoods.

Sit, Robb, Kate said.

He took the other bentwood and, after sitting, pulled a handkerchief out of his shorts pocket and wiped his forehead. He was sweating profusely; there were dark, circular stains under the arms of his pale blue shirt. Every few seconds or so, he'd glance over at Kate, like a worried dog. I figured he was in love with her.

Men fell in love with her all the time. She wasn't interested in most of them, though there were some she fell for. There was a bald, fat TV executive named Quinn, who Kate used to call every two hours; she'd be in hell if she didn't hear back from him at least twice a day. She made his life miserable. I'd go out with them sometimes; we'd sit in expensive restaurants, the kind that served baby carrots and baby corn and different kinds of water at five dollars a glass, and Kate would start in on him.

You're a bastard, she'd say.

It would usually have to do with him choosing his job over her. She was always trying to get him to sacrifice his work time for her, though his work was what gave him a claim to being an interesting guy.

I think you're being damned unreasonable, he'd say.

You said you'd cancel.

You said you didn't want to come.

I *assumed* you'd cancel, she'd say.

I thought you'd love to go, he'd reply. Everybody wants to get in, and I got us in.

I wasn't feeling well.

That doesn't change the fact that I had to go.

You did not make that clear.

I had to go, he'd say. It was work.

You did not make that clear. You deliberately did not make that clear so that I would stay home alone. So that I would not make plans.

Why would you want to make plans if you were sick? he'd ask.

I am not your bimbo, she'd say. I am not your blow-up doll.

Around that point, she'd bolt, dragging me with her, my eyes full of him sitting there among all the half-empty plates, fork suspended, mouth hanging open, looking like a dope. An hour later she'd be on the phone with him at her apartment, crying, saying, *It's because I love you so much;* and I'd be sitting in a chair listening to her and shuddering, mainly from recognition. Our styles were different but the content was much the same: Unhappy unless in hell; in hell unless unhappy.

She sat in my room now, surrounded by three men, and raised her glass.

To the host, she said. The host with the least.

That's not nice, Paul said.

I meant the furniture, Kate explained. The externals. Otherwise he's as full as anybody.

She turned to me and smiled.

Robb made a strange sound, halfway between a bark and a squeak. I thought he'd hurt himself. When I looked over, I realized that he was laughing. He had a big grin all over his face, which almost wiped out the rest of his small features. He gulped some champagne, took his handkerchief out of his pocket again, and wiped his forehead. His eyes were very bright, even in the dark; bright blue.

You're sweet to laugh when I'm not funny, Kate said to him.

No I'm not, Robb said. You *are* funny.

What did you think I meant? Kate asked. What did you think I was saying?

Robb looked confused. He shrugged, tilting his glass and spilling wine over his hand. He put his fingers to his mouth and licked them. Kate continued to stare at him, keeping him on the spot. Finally, he said,

I don't know. It just sounded funny, after all. Hey.

Hey, Paul said.

Hey, Kate repeated.

Robb shrugged again, and they laughed at him. I don't think he knew. Or if he knew, maybe he didn't care. And if he didn't, why should I? It occurred to me that to actually know someone was a miracle.

I decided to get drunk.

More, I said, holding out my glass.

The mountain is moving, Kate said.

Look out, Paul said.

Robb shifted in his chair, reaching down for another champagne bottle at his feet. He opened it, poured another round. We raised our glasses. We drank to each other, we drank to the furniture, we drank to the lack of it. We drank to the scalding heat, untempered by the rain.

I'm glad you left, Kate said to me. This is better. If you'd stayed we'd never have come.

We'd never have come if you hadn't insisted, Paul said to her.

I wouldn't have insisted if you hadn't said no, Kate replied.

I said yes, Robb said.

You did, Kate said, reaching over and patting his leg. You said yes.

I said it was late, Paul said. I didn't say no.

Paul doesn't miss you the way I do, Kate said to me. He's a shallow man. Only loves himself.

You're a bitch, Paul said. Why are you a bitch?

He got up from the mattress, and made for the bathroom.

The door doesn't close right, I called after him.

I know, he said. I remember.

He doesn't remember, Kate said. He didn't think this was the right place at all.

Yes he did, Robb said.

Whose side are you on? Kate asked him.

Nobody's, he replied.

He's about truth, I said.

Don't start, old man, Kate said. Can I have a cigarette?

All gone, I said. The rain got them.

I left my cigarettes in the car, Kate said.

I'll get them, Robb said.

He started to get up.

Don't bother, Kate told him.

It's no bother, he said.

No, don't, Kate said. Really.

Really, he insisted. I need some air. No offense, but it's a little stuffy.

It's small, I agreed.

I have to keep my head clear, he said. It's a long drive.

Ass, Kate whispered.

What? Robb said.

He slapped his hand over his mouth and rolled his eyes. It was something out of a silent movie, except he was completely unconscious of it.

The damage is done, Kate told him.

Sorry, he replied.

What's going on? I asked.

We're going away and we want you to come, Kate said.

I'll get those cigarettes, Robb said.

He shambled out into the kitchen. We heard the door open and close behind him.

You leaving, Bob? Paul called. Are we going?

The water ran in the bathroom, and Paul came back into the room. He stood at the foot of the mattress, next to his sister.

Where did Bob go? he asked.

Robb, Kate said.

Bob, Robb, Paul said. Where'd he go?

Cigarettes, I said.

That's good of him, he replied.

He stood for a minute, brushing his hand through Kate's hair. They looked nice together, just then, affectionate.

So where is it you're going? I asked.

What do you mean? Paul asked.

New Jersey, Kate said. We were going to spring it on you. Robb had to go and say something.

Did he? Paul asked.

Just now, Kate said, when he walked out.

Loose lips, Paul said. Have something more to drink.

He poured me another glass of wine.

He has an enormous cottage out there, Kate said. A house. On a lake. Robb and his brother have it. And his boyfriend.

Robb's? I asked.

No, his brother's, Kate replied. Mickey.

George, Paul said.

No, Kate corrected. That's the boyfriend.

That's what I meant, Paul said. The boyfriend. George.

Right, Kate said.

Have something more to drink, Paul repeated, and filled my glass again, though it was not even half empty. He poured another for himself and Kate.

Hot in here, isn't it? he said. How do you stand it so hot?

The lake is beautiful, Kate said. Cool and green. I've been there twice already.

Wait a minute, I said.

The buzzer rang: Robb, returning with Kate's cigarettes. I got up from my chair and buzzed him in, and stood in the kitchen looking at Kate and Paul sitting together on the mattress, drinks in their hands, watching me, grinning.

No, I said. Absolutely not. No. Sorry.

I told you he wouldn't, Paul said.

You were right, Kate said.

Sorry, I said, again.

Robb opened the door a little and poked his head in.

Knock knock, he said.

This is the place, I said.

He looked very happy with himself. I imagined that he'd done some sort of deep-breathing exercise on the front stoop to clear his head, completely oblivious to the threat of desperate addicts, waiting for some innocent like him to come along. It was an unfair image, probably, but I enjoyed it. He held the cigarettes aloft in one hand, and another bottle of champagne in the other.

Look what I found, he said, passing me, and going into the other room and laying his treasures down in front of Kate.

What a hero, she said.

She kissed him on the lips and gave him a big hug.

My hero, she said.

I stayed in the kitchen. Paul opened a third bottle of champagne, poured Robb a glass and refilled his own. He came into the kitchen to refill mine, and stood so close I could feel his body heat radiating from him in waves. He told me, while Kate and Robb sat whispering in the other room, how glad he was to see me again and that I was looking very well. I reminded him that it was the middle of the night and fairly dark and, on top of everything else, we were now sort of drunk, so he could have no real idea how I looked. But he insisted that I looked very well. He put his arm around my shoulder, took a slug out of the champagne bottle, and then leaned in even closer and said in a low voice that he thought I really should come with them, that it would be a very friendly thing to do. Kate wasn't sleeping nights anymore, he told me; she needed to have a good

friend around. She'd taken their father's death very hard. I
said she had Robb, and he seemed solid enough. But Paul
said what she needed was a real friend, someone who knew
her well enough.

Well enough for what? I asked.

To take it, Paul answered. To take some of the pressure
off me.

I took a step or two away from him.

You really are a shallow man, I said. Christ.

He sighed.

I'm sorry, he said, I don't mean it like that. I take it back.

You can't take it back, I said. Not once it's said.

I went back into the other room, where Robb was sitting
on the bed with Kate. They were both smoking, using an
empty champagne bottle as an ashtray. Robb had his arm
around Kate's neck. They were both sweating; their faces
were streaked with it. I picked up the pack of cigarettes and
shook one out.

I'm sorry the fan doesn't work very well, I said.

That's all right, Kate said. We'll be going soon.

She looked worn out. It was late.

It's not like there's anything you can do about it, she
said. Horrible heat.

Yes, I agreed. Not much you can do.

Except last it out, she said.

I pulled a hand across my face and wiped it on my running shorts. There was so much sweat, it left a stain. I was
having difficulty breathing; I was drunk, now, but there
was no euphoria. In the dim light, Kate and Robb and Paul
started to look hazy and indistinct. The sky was still dark.
It would be another couple of hours before dawn.

Is he coming with us? Robb asked.

No, Kate replied. He won't come. Too busy or something.

That's too bad, he said.

I don't think he was brokenhearted. Actually, he looked relieved.

We should go then, Paul said.

Yes, we should go, Kate said.

Up we go then, Robb said.

He stood up and pulled Kate to her feet. She came up lightly, easily, as if unfolding. Paul came in and collected the empty champagne bottles, and carried them out into the kitchen.

It was nice of you to stop by, I said to Kate.

Well, she replied, we tried.

Do you mind if I have some water? Robb asked.

Not at all, I said. It comes out white, though.

Water isn't water anymore, Paul said. Have you noticed?

Robb went to the sink and turned on the tap. He let it run a little bit before filling his glass. He drank three glasses, gulped them down in succession.

Good Christ, Kate whispered to me. Moby Date.

Don't, I said.

We went into the kitchen and said good-bye.

You don't have any cigarettes, do you? Kate said.

No, I replied.

She shook out three from the pack that Robb had brought up.

Take these, she said.

No, I told her. I can wait.

No, honestly, she said. Take them. You never know. It's late.

She held out the cigarettes in her open palm, a fragile gesture that made my head hurt. I turned away from it and looked into her face: Her eyes were circled with tiny lines. Just as earlier in the night, with Vivitski's girl, I had now a terrible feeling of remorse, without having actually done anything to cause it.

All right, I told Kate. I'll come.

She smiled at me.

How about that? she said. How about that?

You won't regret it, Robb said, sounding less relieved than before.

No, Paul said.

It's green and beautiful, Kate said. Just the thing.

I glanced at Paul, but he looked away. What the hell, I thought, he was probably just embarrassed.

Let me get a few things together, I said.

No, don't pack, Kate said. You'll change your mind.

Shoes, I said. A shirt. My wallet.

Just those things, Kate said.

Robb went down to start the car and Paul went with him. Kate leaned against the kitchen wall, watching me tie my tennis shoes and find a clean shirt to put on.

I'm glad you're coming, she whispered.

Me, too, I said. Me, too, I guess.

After I locked the door, I remembered that I hadn't dumped the ashtrays, or thought to take my toothbrush and razor. But Kate wouldn't let me go back in. She pulled me down the hall. As we got outside, she started singing,

The farmer in the well. The farmer in the well! Heigh-ho the dairy-o the farmer in the well!

Dell! Paul shouted from the front seat of the car. It's dell; not well.

What's a dell? she shouted back to him.

I don't know! he shouted back. But it isn't well.

The farmer isn't well! Kate sang. *The farmer isn't well! Heigh-ho the dairy-o! The farmer isn't well!*

An old woman yelled from one of the dark windows that

looked onto the street, *Keep it down!* In reply, Robb pressed hard on the car horn. Kate and I pushed into the back seat as he gunned the motor, honked again, and pulled away from the curb. Air rushed in through the windows, moist and cool. In less than twenty minutes we were speeding across the George Washington Bridge. Robb drove fast; I hadn't pegged him for a daredevil. He drove so fast, I started to get worried. The pavement was very wet after the rain, and there were a lot of puddles. We slid, a couple of times.

Oh God, old man, Kate said next to me. The farmer isn't well. The farmer may just puke. Tell us a joke, old man.

I can't think of any, I said.

Hold me down, then, she replied. So I don't do anything.

I held her next to me in the back seat. Her head was very close to mine.

Do you remember, she whispered, I had three wishes at your door?

Yes, I whispered back.

My third wish was that you'd come, she said.

That's nice, I told her.

I missed you, old man, she said.

Hell, I said. I missed you, too.

We crossed the bridge and rode the turnpike in silence for a while. Paul suggested that we open another bottle of champagne and reached back to get one. I looked out the window. The city, shrinking steadily in the distance, burned against the eastern sky. I turned away again just before its pointed glow was swallowed up by darkness.

PART TWO

5

THERE WERE KIDS PLAYING under my window. Not
city kids — there was something wild in their voices, an
impoliteness, a sound untamed by dangers lurking. I was
all tangled up in the sheets, and sweat clung to me like an
old skin, a persistent, irritating itchiness. The heat was
here, too. There was a scent of growing things, all right —
trees, grass, the smell of fresh water — but the air was just
as heavy, just as thick as what we'd left behind — dizzying,
intoxicating air.

The children drifted away.

I fell back to sleep.

When I woke up a second time there was an intruder in my
room, banging around in the dresser drawers, looking for
something. I raised myself on one elbow and watched him. I
didn't ask what he was doing; I couldn't get my voice to
work.

The room was hot, and flooded with light. I couldn't
remember ever having been so dry. I was drenched in
sweat, but dry inside.

Good morning, the intruder said, when he saw me
watching him. Good afternoon.

'Ello, I whispered.

He stared at me, leaning against the dresser. The look on

his face made me understand the word *sheepish:* innocent, dumb, embarrassed, and strangely pleased all at once. He looked young, about twenty or so, and he was tall and skinny, with long wavy brown hair and dark eyes. He had on a pair of baggy white shorts but no shirt. Sandals. Long feet. His chest and bony knees were pink; not someone who'd been out in the sun a lot.

I was sent to wake you up, he said.

Why? I asked. Who?

Your friends, he said. I heard you come in this morning. I'm your roommate. Andrew.

My head hurt. I sat up slowly. Light was streaming into the room from two windows. I had to squint.

I was very, very hung over.

Our safe arrival, an hour before dawn, had been celebrated out on the dock behind the cabin. Robb was all for going for a swim, but we had all had too much, so we nixed the idea, and instead sat out in the pre-auroral glow and drank some more; there were only two bottles left by then. Just after sunrise, Kate and Robb went in to bed, and Paul and I had the last bottle by ourselves. He took my hand at one point, and tried to say some things to me, but I told him to quit; he was always aggressive when he drank, and he never meant what he said. I left him on the dock and went to bed.

I didn't remember seeing anybody when I got up to the room. I didn't remember coming up to the room. It was all blank after I left Paul on the dock. I didn't recall anyone saying that I'd have to share a bed. Fortunately, it was a big bed.

I asked Andrew what time it was.

After two, he told me.

I groaned and leaned my head against the wall and closed my eyes. Dry as I was, I wanted a smoke. Andrew was staring at me; I could feel it.

I opened my eyes.

Has my face turned green? I asked him.

No, he replied. Why?

Could you look somewhere else for a while, then? I asked. It's a lot, right now.

He flushed scarlet; a nice trick, I thought.

There's coffee still, he said. I could bring you coffee.

I squinted at him. He liked me; in that, he was not very subtle. I didn't want to take advantage of him. However, there are some things in life, some times in life: Nothing personal.

I would be very grateful, I replied. I would bless your children. And your children's children.

It's no big thing, he said, going to the door. How do you take it?

Light, I said. Very light. No sugar. The bitter the better.

Right, he said.

He opened the door.

Andrew, I said.

He stopped.

Yes? he replied.

If you could find a cigarette. Even half a cigarette . . .

I'll try, he said, and ducked out of the room.

I swung my legs out of bed and sat for a while, getting used to being upright. It didn't seem worth the effort; the advantage was lost on me just then. I scanned the floor. Curiously, I couldn't see my clothes anywhere. They had to be in a corner somewhere, I thought, under the bed, in the closet. I didn't remember undressing the night before. I wanted a cigarette very badly now. I took a deep breath and stood up.

It wasn't so bad, once I got used to it. I walked around the room, even bent down, which was no small victory. But I couldn't find my clothes, and the room was not large. I searched the drawers; they were all empty. There was only dust under the bed. I could hear my mother in the room, saying pointless things, asking where I'd left them, telling me that things don't disappear. She always made me crazy when she tried to help. And she was wrong. Things do disappear. That's a basic rule of life. Things vanish without a trace.

I was standing in the middle of the room when Andrew came back with the coffee. His face turned bright red when he saw me, naked and muttering to myself. There was something about his blushing that I didn't like, but I wasn't sure what it was. Getting caught like that was embarrassing. I pretended it didn't matter. I took the cup from Andrew, thanked him, and went to sit on the bed. He stood stock still in the door frame, not knowing where to look. I asked him if he'd seen my clothes. He looked around, confused.

Your clothes? he asked.

Yes, I said. Fig leaves. My skins.

No, he said.

Oh well, I replied. Just a thought.

Sorry, he said.

I sipped my coffee while Andrew watched me. I felt obliged to talk, but I didn't want to. There was too much light in the room, too much heat. I was uncomfortable and itchy from sweat. Andrew blushed again in the silence. I couldn't put my finger on what bothered me about it.

Did you find any cigarettes, maybe? I asked him.

Yes, he replied.

He reached into the pocket of his shorts and pulled out a brand-new box. That made me very happy. He went through the ceremony of removing the cellophane, flipping open the top, and shaking the pack. It took a long time, as he was not very expert, and I had a few desperate thoughts as I sat watching him. Finally, he offered the pack to me, and I pulled a cigarette out while he extracted a lighter from his pocket and flicked it, almost burning the end of my nose. I breathed in the smoke too deeply at first, and got a little dizzy.

They were sent up for you, Andrew said when the whole process was completed.

Thanks, I said. Who?

Who? he repeated.

Who sent them? I said.

Oh, he said. Your friend. The girl.

My friend the girl is a very good friend, I said.

I inhaled gratefully and held the smoke in my lungs, which gave me a very pleasant sense of being real, a sense of groundedness. I started to feel more peaceful, and I didn't mind Andrew so much. The smoke made a kind of wall, a boundary where I left off and he began; I tilted my head and watched it rise.

We went to town this morning, Andrew said. Your friend and me. She's nice.

She's a peach, I agreed.

She likes you a lot, he said. You can tell.

We're a peach of a pair, I replied.

I believe in astral twins, Andrew said.

Do you? I asked. What is it you believe about them?

That everybody has one, he said, and is destined to find him.

He smiled and looked away; I felt suddenly powerful over him.

I have to think about that, Andrew, I said at last. The big question for me would be, would my astral twin have any money? Because if he didn't, I'd rather he just stayed in the ether. Or wherever.

He didn't say anything right away. I wasn't sure if I'd hurt his feelings or not, though I thought I'd be doing him a good turn if I had.

I didn't say you had to believe, too, he said finally.

That's true, I said. Funny. First thing in the morning and I shit on people's bright ideas.

It's not morning anymore, he said.

That's true, I said. That's true, too.

Sure, he replied.

He went back to his post at the dresser. *Thoughtless violence, one — innocent bystander, zero.*

I heard the kids again, coming closer. They were laughing. Kate was with them, and called to me from outside one of the windows.

Rip, she called. Rip Winkle wake up!

Leave me alone, I called back to her.

Rapunzel, Rapunzel, let down your long hair, she shouted; the kids took up the chant.

Come to the window, Kate said.

No, I said.

We have a surprise, Kate said.

Better be good, I said.

Oh, it's good, Kate said. It's a good one.

I got up, taking the sheet with me to cover myself. I stood off to one side of the window, but even so, it was hard not to blink. The sun was so bright. An unaccustomed world was out there, slender trees bending and branches shaking, casting shadows in spiral patterns; a world of light, fresh colors, and dappled things. In the middle of it were three blond children and Kate, hopping up and down. They had my clothes.

Come and catch us! Kate said.

Bring those back, I said.

They shook their heads and ran away; only their laughing answered me. I turned back into the room. My head was throbbing.

My friend the girl is a bitch, I muttered.

Andrew was leaning against the dresser, arms crossed, very red now, and looking away.

Were you part of this? I asked him.

He nodded.

That's nice, I said. Thank you.

I went back to the bed and sat down and finished my coffee. The room seemed to have become very stuffy. I wanted to get out.

I don't guess you have anything I could borrow? I asked Andrew. You, or your astral twin.

I'm not supposed to, he said.

I nodded again and looked for somewhere to tip my cigarette ash. The floor was the only place. What the hell, I'd clean it up later. I must have looked very upset right then. Andrew said he'd give me something to wear.

That won't interfere with anything, will it? I asked. Breaking promises? That won't send tidal waves through your karma?

No, he said.

He was smiling; if I'd upset him before, he'd gotten over it. Innocent bystander, one.

Good, I said. I would appreciate it, Andrew.

He blushed again, and then it came to me. Blushing is only attractive on people you're attracted to.

I didn't shave, and I cleaned my teeth with toothpaste on my finger. Andrew left a pair of drawstring shorts on the bed; pink, loud, not what I would have chosen; he left a couple of T-shirts, too, for me to choose from. I felt like a fool, dressed in his clothes, and sweating, even after a cold shower. I couldn't shake the feeling of being just a little dirty.

I heard voices on the porch when I went downstairs, so I went outside. I was hungry, but I had to be polite. It was hotter out there than it was inside. Kate was standing with her back to the lake, smoking a cigarette. She looked very pretty, and completely untouched by the previous night's drinking. There were two men with her, one of whom was sitting at a little wrought-iron table in one corner of the porch. The other sat on a glider next to the screen door, and next to him was a boy of about four, eating a Popsicle — one of the three kids I'd seen earlier. They stopped talking when I came out.

You were supposed to come out wrapped in a bed sheet, Kate said. The children were all prepared to meet an ancient Roman.

The ancient part was right, I said.

Betrayed me, she said. First thing.

She kissed me on the cheek.

You look gruesome, she whispered. Where did you get those awful pants?

She introduced me to the two men. The one sitting at the table was Robb's brother, Mickey. He was short and round, like Robb, but his hair was more of a blond color, and he was better looking. He told me he was very pleased I could make it down, and I thanked him for his hospitality. He said he was delighted; so was I, I said. The man sitting on the glider was Jack Vine. He and his wife had the cabin next door on the right. They were from Morristown. The little boy's name was Sam. He pressed himself closer to his father and concentrated on his Popsicle. Jack was about forty, maybe forty-three, a beefy sort of guy with thinning yellow hair and a big nose. He was very red. A likely candidate for a stroke, I thought. We said how do you do, but nothing came back at me through his eyes.

Come look, Kate said to me, after we'd made small talk. She pulled me down the stairs down into the yard.

Isn't it beautiful? she said.

The lake was directly ahead of us, and the dock where we had rung in the morning. Far away, I could make out the other shore; there was a hill, lined with dark green trees, fir, probably. The water caught the light of the sun, and its surface shimmered and glowed white. It was brilliant, glaring. Under the trees surrounding the cabin, the world was mercifully darker. Rusty pine needles covered the ground, and flower heads, bits of birds' nests, acorns.

It's beautiful, I said. Yes.

We walked out onto the dock and looked into the water. We could just see our reflections, distorted and torn by ripples of white light.

I wonder if that's how we look to the fish, Kate said.

She searched for something in her pockets.

I don't have my cigarettes, she said.

You sent some up to me, I said.

That's right, she said.

It was thoughtful, I said.

I try, she replied. Most times.

I took the pack from my pants pocket and shook two cigarettes out of it. I gave Kate one, and lit them both off the same match.

We need a third, she said. For luck. Three on a match.

Three on a match is bad luck, I told her.

Is it? she asked.

I noticed that her hand was shaking, and said so.

I'm hung over, she said, tipping her ash.

Where's Robb? I asked. He must have had a pretty head when he woke up.

He's fishing somewhere, she replied. With George, Mickey's partner.

His what?

That's what they call each other, Kate said. Partner.

Very polite.

I think that's the intention. I think the intention is not to offend.

We smoked for a minute or two, looking out over the water, thinking about Mickey and George.

Whaddya say, Pardner? I said.

Whaddya say? Kate replied.

It was very hot and still. The sun was burning up the sky. Sweat ran down my forehead and into my eyes.

Paul is out there with them, Kate said. Imagine Paul, fishing.

Not easy, I said.

Just below the water's surface, I could see a few fish swimming back and forth, trying to catch the insects breeding in the shadows of the dock pilings. In order to live, one thing had to devour another; that was a lousy deal. But there was no way around it. Nothing personal.

Who's this Robb? I asked.

We've known each other some time, she said. Six months.

What's the idea? I asked.

I'm happy, she said.

Well, that's good.

Aren't you going to say congratulations? she asked.

No.

Why not?

I flicked my cigarette into the water. It made a faint hissing noise when it struck. I turned to face Kate.

Is that why you brought me out here? I asked.

I'd be happy for you, she said.

You would.

I want you to be happy for me.

I shook another cigarette out of my pack and lit it. I suddenly felt very light, insubstantial. I was dizzy, from the heat.

I don't believe you, I said.

You don't want to believe me, Kate said.

I don't believe you, I repeated.

There was some commotion in the trees off to the right, and the two other children I'd seen earlier broke through. Kate turned around and waved to them. A blond, plump woman came out after them, carrying a six-pack of beer. Their mother, I guessed. Kate walked off the dock toward them; I followed and she introduced me. Heidi Vine said she was glad to meet me finally, since she'd heard a lot about me from Kate. I didn't know how to respond to that. I couldn't help thinking what a stupid thing that was to say to someone; it puts them in the terrible position of having to say something banal or untrue, or leaving an awkward silence. I hadn't heard a damn thing about her. I ended up saying how nice it was to make her acquaintance. It didn't sound right, though. It sounded like a lie.

Tina, the older of the two girls, pulled at Kate's leg and whined at her to play a game; right away, I didn't like Tina. She was a mousy kid, who would probably grow up to be a snippy adult. The other girl was about six years younger, and she was a beauty. Her name was Melissa. When Kate and Tina ran off to collect Sam, she stayed right by her mother.

Go on, Melissa, Heidi said to her. Go play.

The girl stared up at her mother with very wide eyes, as if she were very surprised, or disappointed. She wandered after the others, frowning.

Kids, Heidi said.

She took a pull on the beer in her hand.

Want one? she asked me.

Yes, I said. Thank you.

Be my guest, she said.

Don't mind if I do, I said.

We walked towards the house together. Only Jack was still sitting on the porch. Kate and the kids were running off into the woods. I wondered where Mickey had gone.

Heidi waved to her husband.

Hi, she said. Wee-oo.

When we got up the stairs, she kissed him on the top of the head and lowered herself onto the glider, next to him. It swung a little under her weight. Jack didn't acknowledge her at all. That was unpleasant. I leaned against the porch railing, and half looked out at the lake. There wasn't much else to see, except the trees on either side of the property. At my feet was a pile of worn-out comic books.

Sometimes we get an old sea gull or two out here, Heidi informed me.

Really? I asked.

After it rains, she said. I don't know why. Maybe they smell the sea in the rain.

Could be, I said.

Aren't you hot? she asked Jack. I'm so hot.

She offered him a fresh beer. He didn't say anything, but he took the beer. Heidi shifted a little, and raised her right hip. She slid her hand underneath her and pulled out a Popsicle stick.

For Christ's sake, she said. Did you let him eat a Popsicle, Jack?

Yeah, Jack said.

He wouldn't eat his lunch, Heidi said. I told him he couldn't have a snack if he wouldn't eat his lunch.

It's hot, Heid, Jack said. Let him eat what he wants.

Spare the rod and spoil the child, Heidi said.

The heat's a bitch, Jack said, addressing me directly for the first time.

Yeah, I agreed.

What do *you* do? Heidi asked me.

I'm an actor, I said.

There's a hard life, she said.

Yes, I said. I guess it is.

Have you done anything famous? she asked. Would I know you?

Mainly plays, I said. Mainly out of town. I was on public television last year.

We watch public television, Heidi said. I love the narrator on the English program. Very *distinguished*.

He's a fag, Jack said.

Heidi looked upset. I didn't think it was for my sake, or because Jack contradicted her. I had a quick, distinct impression that that was how she registered attraction.

I always wanted to *be* an actress, Heidi continued. I was in a play in high school. I loved it. The costumes. Jack's in insurance. Like Mickey and Robb. They're in insurance, too.

I looked at Jack fairly brightly and asked, Life?

Banks, Jack said. Investments.

Ah, I said.

Something quivered around Jack, some preoccupation. He wasn't all there.

We rented an awful place last year, Heidi said. North of here about twenty miles. It was just awful. We're so much happier here.

Really? I asked.

She had a way of being animated without moving very much and it made me want to laugh. Her eyes moved, and so did her forefinger, digging the nail into her thumb. But none of the rest of her moved. She was like a doll. Pull the string and she talks. Pull the string and she rolls her eyes.

Why was it awful? I asked.

Oh, the people, she said. They were old and boring. It's nicer here. Having people our age around. Like they say in England — People Like Us.

She thinks she's the queen, Jack told me, smiling, sharing a choice bit with me.

I do not think I'm the queen, Heidi said.

She thinks she's queen, Jack repeated.

I like to have fun, Heidi said. Not like *some* people.

Here we go, I thought. *Oh boy.*

You should meet the Hazletts, Heidi said. In the cabin on the other side of us. Stevie and Phil. They're nice, a beautiful couple.

A handsome couple, Jack said, looking out over the lake.

They're trying to have children, Heidi said. Confidentially speaking.

Jack finished his beer. He asked me if I was ready for another, but I said I wasn't yet. He nodded and leaned over, reaching into the cooler next to his chair, his belly squashing against his knees; he breathed through his mouth. When he sat back up, he smiled and heaved a sigh and cracked open the beer can. His smile was like a little kid's. There was something goofy about it, something slack. Heidi rubbed her hand over his thick arm.

Kate kept calling you the old man, she said to me. We thought you might be her ex-husband or something.

Not as far as I know, I said.

She's a nice girl, Heidi said. She and Robb are a good couple.

A nice girl, Jack said, nodding.

I picked up a comic book from the floor of the porch and started to fan myself with it. I had an urge to laugh, for no reason. It was burning hot, and I hadn't eaten anything.

You went out together, though, Heidi said. You and Kate.

No, I said. We're friends, just friends.

You didn't go out?

No, I said. I'm a fag.

Jack looked away. I couldn't help myself. Heidi squinted. That's funny, she said.

The kids ran into the clearing, pumping on little legs, beautiful, lively and intent. Kate came after them on all fours, growling like a bear. I watched them and thought, *Yes, it's funny. A laugh riot.*

You should go for a swim, Heidi said to me. You're sweating bad.

6

IN MY EARLY DAYS of living in New York, a roommate took me around with three of his friends to one of those 25¢ peepshow palaces that line Eighth Avenue. I would never have gone in alone. I was afraid of what might go on there.

The main floor was given over to pictures and movies of naked women. We went downstairs, where there were racks and racks of magazines with obvious titles, and pictures of men that didn't stimulate so much as they amazed. I still can't get some of them out of my mind.

There were about a dozen or so men standing around under the hot white fluorescent lights, thumbing through magazines, staring at the pictures and, more furtively, at each other. That part of it more or less conformed to my expectations; what surprised me was how ordinary they all looked. I had always expected the men in these places to look different — charged somehow, hungry, erotic. Maybe grotesque, or sad. Instead, they might have been anybody's brother or uncle or father. They probably were.

Nobody talked, which surprised me, too. It was a little underground world without sound; a silent movie. Even my roommate and his friends, joining the other men at the racks or around a big table in the middle of the room, browsed in silence.

An old black man, wearing an apron with big pockets

full of quarters, stood by the cashier's counter. After going through the magazines for a while, my roommate went over to him and changed some bills. He beckoned, and handed me a stack of change, then went out through a door at the far end of the magazine room. I followed him into a long corridor lined with booths. It was a lot darker there. Men paced back and forth watching each other more conspicuously. A big sign on one wall said *No Food or Beverages In Booths, Single Occupancy Only! — The Management.* My roommate found an empty booth, tapped on the open door, and pointed at me to enter. I went in and closed the door behind me. The booth was about three feet by three feet; very little room to negotiate. There was a small TV screen directly in front of me, set into the wall, and to the side of it a slot and some buttons. Behind me, a seat was hinged to the wall. I lowered it and sat down after putting a quarter in the slot. The lights went out in the booth, and onto the screen splashed a scene of a reasonably handsome blond man splayed across a bed with a less-good-looking dark-haired man on top of him. Thumping, unvarying music beat in the background, begging someone to dance, to boogie, to party. *Let's make love all night. Give me what I long for.* Every once in a while one of them moaned or said, *Oh yeah.*

One of the great mysteries collapsed for me as I watched. All the grinding and fumbling, sweating and groaning, seemed more farcical than profane: banal.

But I was driven to it. When the screen went blank after a few minutes, and the lights in the booth came back on, I had to see more. I stood up and put another quarter in the slot; the screen lit up again and the booth went dark. As I sat back down, I noticed a small, Plexiglas window in the wall, at about the level of my knee. I bent down to look through it. Another face was pressed against the little window, looking in. I had to slap a hand over my mouth, so as not to scream. It was an experience out of my childhood terrors.

I have always been afraid of looking out a window and seeing another face staring in, the face of some escaped convict or lunatic, who would wave a hatchet or carving knife at me before moving off to cut the power lines. It wasn't being murdered I was scared of — not dying — not the pain of being stabbed or shot or splintered; I've heard that unconsciousness takes over fairly quickly. I'm afraid of that split-second of locking eyes. Suddenly, all my boundaries would be gone — like the moment when all the lines are cut, and the lights in the house go out, the phone goes dead, the alarm system fails. I would disappear, converging with the pitch-black violence.

After a minute in my little cubicle, I dropped my hand and breathed again. I was tempted to look through the window again, just to see if that face was real. Except, if it was, then what? We'd have to make a decision.

I turned back to the screen and started switching channels. Soldiers performing fellatio. A man in leather shaving the head of another man chained to a wall. An orgy by a swimming pool. Bikers having anal intercourse on a motorcycle. *That's good. That's real good. I want you baby want you bad.* On and on, till I ran out of quarters.

When we climbed out onto the street again, it seemed strange to be out in the light around people wearing clothes. We walked a few blocks north to a movie theatre, paid at the booth, and went in. Next to the lobby door was tacked a little cardboard sign with a note in magic marker:

DURING THE CURRENT HEALTH CRISIS THE MGMT. KINDLY RE-
QUESTS THAT PATRONS REFRAIN FROM HAVING SEX ON THE
PREMISES.

It might have been a grand little place in the past. As I
got used to the dark, I noticed vestiges of pseudo-classical
design; little niches, columns, gold leaf. We went to stand
at the rail behind the last row of seats. There were about
fifty or sixty men scattered sitting down, and more leaned
against the back wall. On a small screen down front, a few
boys engaged in barely audible dialogue that served un-
handily as the pretext for getting undressed. I wasn't im-
pressed. But the film was not the major attraction. The
major attraction was the troop of men walking constantly
up and down the aisles, trailing relentlessly forward, hunting in the shadows. I couldn't take my eyes off them. Old
men. Young men. Fat. Ugly. Handsome. I was afraid to
look at them; a feeling like vertigo.

I turned around and my roommate and two of his friends
were gone. The third, a man named Lennis, asked me if I
wanted to go upstairs. I said all right, and followed him,
thinking there must be another screening room upstairs, or
a cocktail room or lounge. But there was only a room with a
little more light — the difference between total blackness
and mere penumbra. There were a couple of wicker chairs
huddled in each corner, and big mirrors hanging from the
walls. Men stood around in varying degrees of shadow,
looking, watching, waiting. I couldn't see the others: Lennis said they were in the bathroom. He started off in that
direction and I went after him.

There were men standing around inside, their pants
down to their knees, other men kneeling in front of them.
More men stood around watching, waiting for the right
number to come up. Men with their shirts up, hands press-

ing, creeping up their chests. Anonymous men, men without names. I heard groans, deep breaths. I saw someone go
down in front of my roommate with a movement almost
formal, saw my roommate's face go slack, his eyes closing,
his jaw dropping. He put his hands on top of the other
man's head. In that small, dim room were performed old
rites, rites of going down into darkness, down into waters
where names were lost. I stayed close to the door, unable to
make up my mind what to do. I couldn't tell if it was what I
wanted. I couldn't decide.

A man came towards me, pale, with long hair, and a
forehead and cheekbones that stuck out. The light hit his
face in such a way that I couldn't see his eyes — it was a
moon-face, marked with two dark spots where his eyes
should have been, and a third dark slash that stood for his
mouth, empty as a crater, devoid, even, of lust. If he
touched me, I would become like him.

He came closer, bending down.

The words rushed up from childhood, murmuring, *our
father who art in heaven hallowed be thy name thy king-
dom come thy will be done on earth as it is on earth as it is
on earth as it is in heaven*

Shh, someone said.

Jesus!

Somebody laughed.

I went downstairs. On the screen I watched a narcotic vi-
sion of naked flesh, of body parts and hair, connecting,
unconnecting, reconnecting, hypnotic and not unheroic. I
watched the lines of men, restless, walking up and down
the aisles. I watched desire coming from the same place as
religion or war, nothing personal, a man's gotta do what
he's gotta do. I went outside, and the Saturday sun cut

through me. Four lanes of cabs and trucks were blowing their horns at a car stalled in the intersection, and those that could squeezed around the helpless vehicle, which made things worse. In a doorway next to the theatre, an old, skinny man threw up. I lit a cigarette and headed down the street with no real direction, no place to go. I remembered how, when I was younger, I wanted eyes of some other color: A person can change anything about the way he looks except the color of his eyes. He can cover them up, cap another color over them; that's possible. But the eyes look wrong then, they look dead.

I could cut out my eyes; but then I'd be blind.

So it was with desire.

I found love affairs hard to sustain. I kept wanting more, wanting blood. I'd grown up with a father who talked to God and the ordinary human drama of *hello dear, how was your day? oh it was? that's too bad, they said what? how nice* couldn't compare. It was anonymity of a different order. No hard questions, let's watch TV — or talk about things but not get beyond them, which is one way to stay young: Staying small.

I would become insubstantial in the presence of someone who was complacent, and didn't want more; I would become resentful. My feeling for that person would grow thinner and thinner until finally it was invisible. The whole idea of a private life was a myth; the idea of a comfortable, insulating marriage of two people was absurd. There was always a third term dogging the heels of any couple — a hell of loneliness and anger supposedly cast out by some ritual of choice words. But words can't keep hell out. That's the special revelation of a minister's kid.

I would look at people like Jack and Heidi Vine and

wonder how they kept going. What was it that sustained them through years distending into fat, broken veins, chipped glasses, oat flakes in the morning and crumbs and bits of skin left on the pillow? I couldn't do it. We were meant to live in caves, I'd think sometimes, mating only because we have to; and then going off to hunt, traveling in packs, silently, without remorse.

I thought I'd shocked Jack with what I'd said, but I was wrong. There had been a fast open and closing of the aura around him, a quick peek, that's all; then he immersed himself again. I wondered about what was buried in him, what treasure. The conversations we tried to have didn't go far: Every time he opened a can of beer he offered me one, and I accepted. It was in the way of a challenge. The whole back and forth took on its own momentum.

Later in the afternoon, when the sun started to slide behind the treetops and things started to cool down a little, we went into the water. Jack dove off the dock, his big belly slapping against the water, sending shocks of yellowing light spreading and shimmying across the surface. I jumped in after him. The water was colder than I'd expected, and it went a long way towards clearing my head. It was pretty slimy and green; I couldn't see far under the surface. I kept getting surprised by colder currents. We swam out, stopping and floating, about a hundred yards from shore.

Jack told me about fighting in the last war. The Far East, he called it. He told me about an old man he'd met there, just after being released from prisoner-of-war camp, an old South Vietnamese doctor who talked to him about four essential qualities — hot, cold, moist, and dry — that together made up the four elements. Cold and moist came together as water; hot and dry made fire; cold and dry combined as earth; hot and moist made air. There were no other possible combinations. There was a fifth element, which had no qualities, and was the life of all the other elements.

I know, I said to Jack. I've heard this. Light.

Jack swam farther from the bank, which I didn't like. I like to be where I can touch the bottom. There are too many things in deep water. Even the idea of these things — strange fish, boat wrecks, bones — made me nervous. Jack swam out a little and then looked back, testing my limits. I swam after him: I didn't want to seem weak. I met up with him in the middle of the lake and we stayed there, treading water. Having risen to the challenge made me feel excited.

The sun went lower behind the trees, and I could see more clearly the cabins on the other side of the lake. People were coming out into their yards to light their fires, to light their grills for dinner. Jack and I hung in the middle of the lake, with all of this going on around us. I liked being there, buoyant.

I was in a cage six months in the north, Jack said. This cage was half submerged in water.

I nodded.

There is a particular sound made by men who die in water, he said. When all the air passes out of them.

Did a lot of men die? I asked.

He ignored me.

There's a sound a man makes when he sees a corpse floating up next to him in the morning light, he said. It's the same sound.

I wondered if Jack was going to kill me. I wondered if that was why he'd brought me out there. I stared into the center of a terrible imbalance trying to hold itself together;

a vortex. I stared at a man who carried extremes like Saigon and Morristown inside him, with a rage and a wariness sandwiched in between.

The fifth thing, Jack said, the fifth element is sound. Not light.

Sound, I repeated.

Not light, he said.

We swam back to shore. Jack got there first and was already drying off on the dock when I finally made it. He gave me a hand up, and waited for me to finish drying myself; then we went together back to the porch for more beer.

Towards seven in the evening, Paul and Robb came back from fishing, with a third man, who was introduced to me as Mickey's partner, George. George was tall and dark haired, with little round glasses, and a beard; he had a grayish complexion and a look on his face like he smelled something bad. He was very curt with me, and when we shook, his hand was limp. I wondered what Mickey saw in him.

Heidi and Kate came out from the house.

How was the fishing? Kate asked.

Good, Robb said, opening the basket with a kind of flourish to show us five or six nice-sized fish, wrapped in leaves.

See? he said.

He pulled one out of the basket, holding it by the tail. It slipped out of his hands. He bent over to pick it up, a clumsy operation. Kate frowned, watching him.

Did you like it? she asked Paul.

Yes, Paul said. It was great.

What was great about it? Kate asked.

Fishing is sexy, Robb said, rewrapping the fish he'd dropped.

Fish are sexy, he said.

Oh go on, Heidi said.

We had a big barbecue that night, all of us sitting together at a long picnic table pulled out under the trees, slapping at mosquitoes who defied the citronella candles placed at intervals along the table, their waxy odor rising. Mickey grilled the fish, and everybody else pitched in with other things. Heidi brought over some Jell-O from their cabin. It was a nice, informal meal. Everybody talked at once, reaching past each other, refilling their plates. As the sun went down, the air became marginally cooler and less heavy.

Down at one end of the table, George started in about the garbage washing up along the coast.

I read how there is actually sewage, Heidi affirmed, bending across the table to look at George. That's why we come here. I don't want my kids exposed to that.

Everything costs too much, George said. Even garbage. It's dumped on the sly.

And needles, Heidi said. Can you imagine? You go out for a swim and you step on one of those?

Nobody's above a lie anymore, George said. Every man for himself.

Let's talk about something pleasant, Mickey said.

Morristown is a very nice place to raise children, Heidi said. They have *excellent* schools.

I went to light a cigarette and Sam blew out my match. I squinted at him, sort of a mock threat, and lit another. He blew it out again. I lit another, he blew it out. I growled at

him. He covered his face with his hands. Paul lit a match
behind my back, and Sam leaned across the table to blow it
out. He got his hands in a dirty plate and Heidi smacked
him. He sat back and started to cry.

Crabby Abby, Heidi said.

She reached down the table for a big blue bowl.

Who wants Jello-O? she asked.

Red Jell-O, Sam said.

There's no red Jell-O, Heidi said.

I wish we had canned fruit, Mickey said to Heidi. My
mother used to put canned fruit in Jell-O. Canned fruit
cocktail.

Heidi smiled.

Mine, too, she said.

She smiled.

This heat, George said across the table to Andrew. Global
warming. Acid rain. The ozone. It all comes down to the
same thing.

Andrew nodded. I wondered if George might be his astral
twin. Maybe I'd suggest it to him.

We're running, George said. Running from death. And
now we're falling. Slipping on foolish pride, thinking we
can outrun death.

Do you remember Dream Whip? Mickey asked.

Yes, Heidi said. I wish we had some now.

When algae dies it turns red, George said, the water turns
red. They call it red tides. It's like blood washing up on the
shore.

Red tides in the sunset, Robb sang, sitting next to Kate,
wearing only his bathing trunks. Without a shirt on he
looked very round and white. His pectoral muscles were
flabby.

I wish we could think of something pleasant, Mickey said to George. If you can't say something pleasant, don't say anything at all.

My mother used to say that! Heidi said.

Everybody's mother said that, Robb said.

You can't bury your head in the sand, George said. The more you try to get away from it, the closer it gets. That's been the mistake all along. Pride goeth before a fall.

My mother used to say that, Andrew said.

Jack made no contribution at all to the talk. He ate and drank. He stared at Kate. There was a piece of corn on his cheek, right at the corner of his mouth; it stayed there through the entire meal. Nobody thought to let him know.

Heidi started spooning dessert on Sam's plate.

This is more fun than last year, she said to Mickey. Last year there was no one to talk to, practically.

Red Jell-O! Sam complained.

There is no red Jell-O, Sam, Heidi said. There never was any red Jell-O. There never will be any red Jell-O. It's green Jell-O or nothing.

I have a hard time with Jell-O, period, Robb said. The way it *slides* down your throat.

Oh brother, Tina said, from the other end of the table.

It's made from horse bones, Robb said to her. Ground up horse bones.

Oh God, Tina said.

Tina, Heidi said. You know I don't like you using language.

Sorry, Tina said.

That's better, Heidi said.

We're patsies, George said, victims of our own conceited ideas about ourselves.

I guess we should have stayed in the caves, Robb said. Is that the idea?

Are you Catholic? Heidi asked. You must be Catholic.

No, George said. Why?

We had cousins who were Catholic, Heidi said. They had to believe in original sin, or else the nuns would hit them across the knuckles.

I don't believe it, Mickey said.

It's true, Heidi said.

At least it was original, Robb said.

Whack, Heidi said. Right across the knuckles.

I believe in that, Kate said.

We watched cartoons on Sunday, Robb said. I believe in Bullwinkle.

It sounded like the Catholic belief you're talking about, Heidi said to George. That's what I meant.

Not just Catholic, I said.

Are you Catholic? she asked me.

Hypocrite, I said.

That's *not* a religion, Heidi said.

I'm not a Catholic, George told her. I'm a realist. I'm saying you can't keep the inevitable from happening. And the more you try, the closer you bring it towards you, and the more frightening it is.

Jack stared over the top of his beer can. When Kate glanced at him, he looked away.

Red Jell-O! Sam shrieked.

No, Sam, Heidi said. Green Jell-O! Now do you want any or not?

Sam pressed himself against his father's side, saying nothing. Jack lit another cigarette and looked sidelong at his wife. Kate smiled. Robb put his arm around her shoulder and she told him to take it off because he was all sweaty.

Do you want dessert, or don't you? Heidi repeated.

Sam wouldn't look at her, pressing his face further into his father's arm. Heidi picked up the bowl and held it in mid-air.

Sam, she said. Sam!

Redjelloredjelloredjelloredjelloredjello, Sam shouted, at the top of his voice.

Sam, Heidi said. Goddammit!

Jack reached over and grabbed the bowl out of her hands and threw it on the ground. It was very quick, so quick it was almost funny.

There, he said. Now there's no Jell-O.

He got up heavily from the table and stalked off into the trees, and Sam ran after him. Heidi sat at the table, very quiet, very white. The rest of us looked away, embarrassed, trying to hold ourselves in our chairs, trying to keep from hurtling into the air. The three-year-old, Melissa, knocked over her milk glass.

For crying out loud, Heidi said.

There was a scramble with napkins and moving plates to clean up the mess, and in the middle of it Heidi reached down and picked up the Jell-O bowl from the ground.

At least it isn't broken, she said.

She looked down at the stuff on the ground.

What a mess, though, she said.

Oh, don't worry, Mickey said. The flies will have a field day. They'll think it's manna from heaven.

I'm so sorry, Heidi said.

Don't worry, Mickey said.

It's the heat, she said. He gets cranky when it's like this.

I know, Mickey said. Look at this one.

I don't get cranky, George said.

Like hell, Mickey said. The hell you don't.

Also, Heidi said, lowering her voice confessionally. Things haven't been so hot at work. Things are a little unsettled right now, what with the economic situation. It's a very stressful time.

I know it, Mickey said. Don't I know it.

Very stressful, Robb said.

I've heard that before, I said, under my breath.

Heidi heard me.

What? she asked.

Everybody turned and stared. It was a minute before I could explain.

It's the kind of thing my mother used to say, I said. She was always saying things like that.

Oh, Heidi said.

She smiled, and patted my hand.

It's nice of you to say that, she said.

7

W*E CLEARED THE TABLE* after dark. It was decided that we'd go for a swim. Kate couldn't go because she'd torn her suit; Heidi told her she could use hers, because she wasn't going to go in the water. The only problem was, the suit was at their cottage.

If you want to brave the storm, she told Kate, be my guest. I have no intention of going there right now.

I'm not afraid of storms, Kate said. I was born in a storm.

Were you? Heidi said.

I want to go home, Tina whined.

I'm not going home now, Heidi told her. End of discussion.

I can take her home, Kate said.

If you're going, Heidi said. I have no intention. Not as yet.

Come on, Sweet Pea, Kate said, holding out her hand.

Tina looked at her mother. She had doubts.

Well, go on, if you want to go, Heidi said. If you want to go, go. I'm not gonna hold your hand.

Come on, Kate said. I'll race you.

I don't want to race, Tina said.

She got up from the table, but didn't take the hand Kate

offered. They disappeared into the trees, and we watched them as long as we could. I stayed with Heidi, while the others went down to the water. I didn't feel like horsing around.

Heidi jiggled Melissa on her lap.

Boy, oh boy, she said. Sometimes.

I know, I said. I agree.

It felt good, to sit there in the relative quiet after dinner. I lit a cigarette. The night sky was opaque and thick, and the stars, as they came out, did not twinkle. They burned steadily, the glittering effect lost in the heavy air. The thought crossed my mind that it might never clear again; that it would always be this hot and humid.

You know, Heidi said, I had real Cinderella fantasies when I was growing up.

Did you? I asked.

Yes, she said. Marrying a prince and all that. Maybe not a prince.

There's a lot of stuff we pick up when we're growing up, I said.

Jack's no prince, she said. I do love him and all, but he's no prince.

A lot of unreal expectations, I said.

Sounds floated in off the water, of the five men playing some sort of game. They sounded like they were having a good time.

I know my parents entertained fantasies for us, Heidi said. For my sister and myself. Big white weddings. They had a lot of dreams for us. I was four months pregnant when I married Jack. It wasn't like twenty years ago, we didn't have to go off to some hole-in-the-wall justice of the peace, but they were disappointed, all the same. They'd

bent over backwards to make sure we had things they
didn't have. I think in some ways they intruded a false
sense of security on us.

Maybe a false sense is better than no sense, I said.

I don't know, she replied. Maybe. Did you entertain fantasies when you were little?

Everyone does, I said.

She lowered her voice.

But being gay, she said. Were they Cinderella fantasies or
prince fantasies?

I didn't answer right away, because my fantasies had
been neuter, void of human aspect. I thought about angels.
Like anyone else, I wanted a cure for the idea of being
alone; I wanted days of perfect communication, perfect
peace, perfect order. Like other people, my fear was sudden
helplessness, a free fall through empty space with no one to
touch me or hear me shout. It's what George was going on
about. In the burning air, the dried earth, and poisoned
waters, he caught the punch line to a very old joke: Death is
something embarrassing stuck to your shoe; you try to pull
it off, and it sticks to your hand; you use your teeth, then
your other hand. Pretty soon you're in a knot, more stuck
than before.

There is no escape from what is basically intolerable.
Faster, cleaner, bigger, brighter things give you the illusion
that there's a hope you can buy: power for the common
man. If you drink the right soft drink you will get the girl
wearing the right jeans, and you will both drive off in the
right car, into a blood red sunset caused by a rising toxin
that is the insidious by-product of so much comfort: a
cloud, lighter than a feather, lighter than air, rising and
folding around the world like a downy soft diaper that will

smother all life. That's a good joke — to be smothered by something so light.

I wiped my hand across my forehead and lit a cigarette. Heidi smiled at me.

Well? she asked.

I wanted to be grown up, I said finally. I don't think it went much farther than that.

Did you know? she asked me.

Know what?

That you were . . . the way you were.

No, I said. Not till late. Not till later.

You didn't think about boys?

No. I thought about growing up. Getting away.

You knew you were different.

I knew I had to get away.

Down, Melissa said.

Heidi lifted the child off her lap and set her on the ground.

Play nice, she said.

She opened another beer, and held the can to her forehead between sips. She was sweating as hard as I was. I was starting to regret not going in the water.

If you'll pardon my saying so, Heidi said, I always wondered what drives a person to become a homosexual. Or do you like gay better? So many terms, now . . . But what is it that drives you?

I didn't know what to say; I didn't know. I would like to have. But I didn't think there was an answer. I didn't think there was anything to explain. I looked to the sky — for inspiration, maybe, for help — and I saw that there was no moon. There were stars but no moon. I wondered what happened to the old moon. I looked back at Heidi, who was waiting for a reply.

It's not like a choice, I said. It's not like you wake up one morning and decide what a nice thing it would be.

But is it some kind of lack? she asked. Are you missing something? Like a father figure or something?

Or is it some kind of excess? I replied.

She looked at me, blankly.

I don't get it, she said.

Neither do I, I said. Just shooting the breeze.

Did you have a father figure in your life? she asked.

Yes, I said. Oh yes.

And?

I loved him, I said. And that's the damn truth.

Well, Heidi said. I guess that's not it, then.

She was disappointed.

I guess it's not, I said. Sorry.

I wish there *was* a breeze, she said. I feel like an old towel.

She yawned. We watched Melissa play. The heat didn't seem to bother her so much.

Don't you ever want to have kids? Heidi asked me.

I like kids, I said.

But you don't want to have any?

I don't know. Someday. I doubt it.

I love the way babies smell, she said. Only babies smell that way, and then they stop. They grow up and they don't smell like babies anymore. I hate that.

She looked down at Melissa again.

Don't put pine cones in your mouth, honey, she said. *Bad.*

Melissa looked up at her mother. She had the pine cone

in her hand and looked at her mother, not quite making a connection. Then she opened her mouth in a yawn.

You're tired, aren't you? Heidi said. Tired baby.

She's tired, she told me. We'll be getting along soon.

We sat listening to the crickets. The men in the water had become very serious about their game; they grew quieter and quieter. After a while, we only heard their splashing. Kate came back through the woods.

All's quiet on the western front, she announced.

Where's the bathing suit? Heidi asked.

Kate put her hand up to her mouth and laughed.

I forgot, she said. I completely forgot.

Oh well, Heidi said. You'll get it tomorrow.

I'll get it tomorrow, Kate agreed. Yes.

She reached for my pack of cigarettes, took one, and lit a match. In the light of it her face looked a little puffy.

We were saying about fantasies, Heidi told her. Did you have fantasies when you were growing up? Cinderella fantasies?

All the time, Kate said. I still do. I never stopped.

That's nice, Heidi said. I wish I still did.

Kate sat down on the edge of the table. I have this one recurring Cinderella fantasty, she said. It's my shoe but it doesn't fit. They try and try, and I know it's mine, but it doesn't fit. Something happened between the ball and finding me.

How awful, Heidi said.

When it isn't funny, Kate said. Sometimes it's funny.

We sat watching Melissa, who lay down in the grass and leaves.

So Jack's calmed down, has he? Heidi asked.

Sleeping like a baby, Kate said. And the little ones. They're all three sleeping like babies.

They were all of them cranky, Heidi said. Tired and cranky. It's this darn heat. We thought we'd get away from it, but I guess we didn't.

She looked down at Melissa.

Did we, baby? she said.

Beautiful baby, Kate said. Beautiful.

Yes, Heidi said, yawning. They're sweet when they're young. I wish they didn't have to grow up.

I want to have a baby, Kate said.

You'd be a good mother, Heidi said.

I'd be a terrible mother, Kate said. A silly mother. Dragging them all over the place all the time. Babies need a home.

Heidi yawned again.

So do mommies, she said.

She bent over and scooped Melissa up in her arms, pressing her face in the little girl's hair, inhaling.

Don't we, baby? she said. Don't we?

She stood up, wobbling a bit.

You going to be all right? I asked.

Oh yes, she said. Just forgot how to stand there for a minute.

She laughed.

Well, goodnight, she said.

Well, goodnight, I said.

Goodnight, Kate said.

She took a couple steps away and then came back, leaning into the table, pressing her hip into the side of it to steady herself and balance the weight of the little girl in her arms. She bent her head in close to mine. I could smell the beer on her breath.

One thing I don't understand, she said to me, is why they call it *gay*. Is there a reason?

I don't know, I said. There has to be, but I don't know what it is.

Hm, she said.

Maybe, she said, because there's a lot of going out. A lot of parties. That must be very gay.

That's probably it, I said.

No, she said. But it sounds good. It's good for now.

All right, I said.

Goodnight, she said.

We said goodnight again and watched her leave. Down by the dock, everyone started to climb out of the water. They were all laughing and joking with one another, and the team that won was lording it over the team that hadn't. Kate turned to watch.

I had a nice time with Jack, she said.

No, you didn't, I said.

The citronella candles started to sputter. Kate dropped her cigarette and ground it into the dirt with her toe. The candles went out.

He's fierce as hell, she said.

You didn't do anything, I said.

I didn't say that, Kate replied. I said we had a nice time.

The men came towards us from the dock, laughing and talking. They stood around, dripping, and going on about their game. But the bugs started getting thick, and we all had to go inside.

It was a big cabin, the size of a suburban house almost, though it had a rougher feel, as if outside and inside had never been defined. There were twigs on the floor, and pine needles and bits of leaves. The furniture was battered, and smelled of something not quite kerosene and not quite mothballs. The linoleum was cracked and lined with ground-in dirt. The whole place was filled with castoffs — castoff furniture, castoff lamps, castoff rugs. There was nothing new, from the bed sheets to the decks of cards missing kings and aces, the old board games missing pieces. Everything was worn, well worn, memoried.

Within half an hour of being out of the water, all five men were sweating again. George had a sour look on his face again, and every five minutes or so Mickey asked if he was doing all right, until finally George snapped at him — which left things quiet for a few minutes.

We decided to play poker, not knowing what else to do. Mickey cleared a big, wooden table in the corner, and we sat around it: Mickey, George on his left, Paul next to him, then Andrew, myself, and Kate. Robb sat out the game on the sofa, with a beer and the newspaper. I didn't play particularly well. My mind kept wandering; my head was heavy. I couldn't concentrate. Nobody played well, really. We were passing time, too hot and listless just to talk to each other. Every once in a while, a mosquito lucky enough to find some hole in the screen landed on one of our arms or legs, biting.

Around midnight, Mickey and George said goodnight and went down the hall together to their room. Kate and Robb followed soon after; Andrew went out onto the porch. I stayed at the table with Paul, listening to the crickets outside.

You'd think it'd cool down, I said.

You'd think, he replied.

I started fiddling with the cards, sorting them by suit.

Funny, her going around with a guy like Robb, I said. A light type like that.

Paul made a face.

I don't care, he said. It's her problem.

I guess it is, I said.

You don't agree with me? he asked.

No, I agree with you, I said. I do.

Really?

Yes, I said. Really.

Good, he said. I'm glad. Good.

I was reminded of one of the first photographs Kate had ever taken of him: standing on his toes, arms outstretched, head tilted to the side — a familiar pose — except that his hands were turned up, and on his face, instead of agony, was a smile that could be called radiant. Paul liked to offer the impression that he could give you happiness, but he never liked the people who fell in love with that.

A mosquito buzzed past my ear. I saw it land on Paul's arm, and he slapped at it and missed; a red handprint showed up on his skin. He lingered over his beer, then patted me on the shoulder and said he was going up. I told him I was going to stay up a while longer. He hovered by the door, waiting, then said goodnight, and went upstairs.

When I turned around in my chair, I saw Andrew was standing at the screen door looking in.

It's a beautiful night, he said. Why don't you come out?

No, I said. I've had enough of the outdoors.

You look sad, he said.

Not sad, I replied. Pensive.

Don't be, he said.

Why not? I asked.

He came inside, easing the screen door shut behind him.

Why are you depressed? he asked me.

I'm not depressed, I said.

Do you mind if I ask a personal question? he said.

That wasn't personal? I said.

Forget it, he said, quickly. Never mind.

No, I said. Go ahead.

Never mind, he repeated.

Andrew, I said.

No, never mind, he said. Goodnight.

He started for the stairs.

Well, goodnight, then, I said.

Goodnight, he said.

I bit my lip. It was so easy to hurt people's feelings; it seems to be easiest when you're trying to be kind. Some people have a kind of instinct for it: The person you feel the worst about is always the one who begs and begs to be told the truth. It's better not to get involved at all.

I waited till I thought Andrew was asleep, and then went upstairs. The room was stuffy and dark. Andrew was on the near side of the bed, so I had to go around to the other side. I moved very slowly, trying not to make any noise. I lowered myself as gently as I could. It was too hot to go to sleep. Andrew rolled over on his side to face me.

I'm sorry if you thought I was being too intimate, he whispered. Downstairs.

Oh, Andrew, I said. You were being sweet.

You just look sad all the time, he said.

And you think that if I let you, you can make it all better, I said. Is that right?

I swung around to face him. He had turned his eyes down to the mattress. A drop of something rolled down his cheek and onto the bed. It might have been a tear.

Andrew, Andrew, I said; he was quiet, so I continued.

From my experience, I said, I have the feeling it would

work out the other way around. Do you see? It would turn out the other way. It already has. Look. Right now.

He still wouldn't answer me, but only lay there, with his eyes turned down and his long brown hair falling across the pillow. A lock of it fell, slowly, from the side of his head down across his face; I leaned over and took it between my thumb and forefinger and put it back. I brushed my fingers across his forehead. He looked up at me.

Shit, I thought. *Goddamn*. Whatever I tried would always come down to the same damn thing; whatever I wanted would always end up the same damn way.

I bent down, trying to see another face, a face I wanted there.

I bent down, and closed my eyes.

8

A THICK, *WHITE HAZE* hid the sun from us the next day. It was very humid, and rain threatened, but never came; the waters simply hung in the sky. We waited.

Andrew rolled over in the morning and I could feel him looking at me, trying to extract something from me, a sign, a sound, a stab of real response. But I kept my eyes closed and made my breathing very regular as if I were still asleep. I stayed in bed late, so as not to have to talk to him.

There was coffee still warm on the old gas range when I went down into the kitchen. I was sitting at the table having a cup, when Kate came in.

Don't move, she said. Stay right where you are. I'm serious.

I stopped with coffee cup midway in the air.

Where is it and what is it? I asked between clenched teeth.

It's you, she said.

There was a click and a whir and a flash of light, a dwarf thunderstorm. I turned around and saw her standing in the doorway, practically beaming, holding a big, old-fashioned camera with a round flash reflector. The bulb was now white and crusted.

Don't you love it? she said. George dug this up from downstairs in the basement. It's rich.

She blew on the flashbulb and popped it out. I went back to my coffee.

It's a beaut, I said.

The film is old, she said. Who knows what it will produce? If it will produce. But there's a whole box of it.

She sat on the table and leaned in close.

Hold still, she said. I want to see if I can get your face in the cup. Don't move.

There was a click, whir, and a flash again; this time the eye of the storm. I couldn't see for several seconds afterwards.

I'm blind now, I said.

Good, she said. You will be under my complete control then. I'll lead you around from now on and spell things in your hand.

I raised my free hand and made some signs in the air.

C-A-K-E, I said. It's a word, Helen.

Another flash hit me.

There, she said. All done. *Ecco homo.*

That's nice, I said.

Andrew is a happy boy today, she said.

Well, I said.

You're not, Kate said. If he's happy, you're not.

It's a little early in the day for that, I said.

I've been up for hours, she said. You've been sleeping.

For one of us, it's early, I said. And one of us would appreciate a little milk of human kindness with his coffee, so if the other one can't manage that . . .

I know, she said. It's an old story. I know how it ends, you don't have to tell me. Just answer me something.

If it's short and easy, I said.

What would happen, old man? If you could be happy with an Andrew, Kate said.

Blindness, I said. Fire. Gnashing of teeth.

No, Kate said. The truth.

It wouldn't cross my mind to try, I said.

I sipped my coffee.

Sap, Kate said.

Well, I said.

What's it going to take? she asked. What's it going to take to get the old man back?

Who knocked on whose door in the middle of the night? I asked. You could have left well enough alone.

I didn't want to, she said. Well enough is not alone.

I don't know, I said.

I'll get you back, she said.

You can try, I said.

She opened her mouth to say something more, and then thought differently about it. She just picked up the camera and left the room. When she was gone, I felt relieved.

I made breakfast and ate it as slowly as I could. I thought if I went slowly enough, the day would pass more quickly. I dawdled over cleaning up. When I was finally finished, I went out onto the back porch.

The sky was gray and thick. Hardly a breeze stirred the branches of the trees, which made everything look oddly contained. I was sweating a lot already; the effect of my shower had worn off. It was a terrible afternoon, a sultry, murky Sunday afternoon, the kind I used to try sneaking away from; *bored with the lesson I've been assigned to learn, sneaking out of the house to walk, a boyish thing to do, through the gully behind the neighborhood I live in. My*

*father catches up with me and I turn around with him
and follow him home. He talks to me about discipline, as
he takes down the strap, about self-control; my mother
watches, wordless as usual, and when it's over it is she I
hate. She won't come to me later, to make me feel better, to
distract me, to explain. There's nothing to explain. Her
silence is like air, everywhere, necessary for life. My love is
for my father. Or if not love, at least respect and awe. I
admire the thing that twists him.*

I looked out over the lake. Andrew was in a raft, with
Tina and Sam, pretending to be terrorized by Robb and
Paul, who were swimming around the raft like sea mon-
sters. How could I possibly explain?

Mickey and George were putting up a volleyball net, arguing about which way it should go. They stopped when I
called out hello.

Isn't it a little hot for sports? I asked.

You can let it beat you, Mickey said. You can let it get
you down.

There's coffee on the stove, George said.

I had some, thanks, I said.

There's eggs.

I had some. Do you need any help?

Nope, Mickey said.

Sure? I asked.

Sure, George said.

Go have fun, Mickey said. This is no fun.

That it's not, George said.

They went back to their argument. I was disappointed. I
went through to the front of the house, and in the front
hallway I found my clothes, folded into a neat little pile on

the floor. I picked up my shirt, brushed it off, and put it on. I shoved my feet into my tennis shoes without untying them; then I went out the front door.

I took off down the road to the left. It was actually more of a dirt track than a road, though it was fairly even; most of the larger stones had been cleared out. Across from the cabin, the trees were densely packed and thick with leaves. There were secrets in that wood; I wondered what it would be like if people had stayed in the trees, in the darkness of the green leaves. Quieter, probably. No noise at all. Just silent nights and days.

About a quarter of a mile down the road I came to the Vines' cabin. It was smaller than Mickey's and set a little farther back from the road. Jack's car was pulled up close along the front of the house. I heard women's voices coming from the back and I cut through the trees to see what was what. I didn't call out as I came around the corner of the house, and it was just as well; through the trees, I saw Kate and Heidi and Melissa in the back yard, and Kate was on her knees, taking pictures.

Heidi and Melissa were sitting on the ground. Melissa had her head pressed against the curve of one of Heidi's breasts, her face turned inward. She was shy of the big camera. It was beautiful — the three of them under the lowering sky, the dark leaves, smells of a summer rain waiting. It was a grounded beauty.

That's a little frog, Kate was saying to the little one, trying to get a smile. That's a birdie.

I must confess I feel a little funny doing this, Heidi said. That's a hen, Kate said.

I feel funny sitting here, a little, Heidi said.

I think you're very attractive, Kate said. Not at all funny.

I'm not used to posing, Heidi said. I'm not used to being looked at.

It's a pity, Kate said.

It's being married, Heidi said.

I think you're very attractive, Kate repeated.

I used to be, Heidi said. I let myself go.

She made Melissa sit forward on her lap.

Look at the camera, honey, she said. Smile baby.

That's what I find attractive though, Kate said.

What? Heidi said, resting her chin on her daughter's head. My fat?

You're not fat, Kate said. Shush a minute.

Do you think any of these will come out? Heidi asked. It's so dark out.

I don't know, Kate said. All I know is this is what I like.

Must be nice, Heidi said.

Shush, Kate said.

This is what I like, Heidi echoed.

Watch the birdie, Kate said.

Where? Heidi said, looking all around.

A song came into my head, *Ladybug, ladybug, fly away home.* I didn't feel right standing there, looking in. I slid back through the trees as quietly as I could.

On the main road I met Jack, walking with a man he introduced to me as Phil Hazlett. As Heidi had said, he was a handsome man. He was somewhere between my age and Jack's. Jack invited me to walk with them into town, which was about two or three miles away. He'd had a few already, and was very jovial and red. I was a little leery of him, after the night before. But I said I'd go. I didn't have anything else to do.

I was sweating so heavily that my shirt was stuck to my back. Perspiration stung my eyes.

You should have been here yesterday, I said to Phil. Yesterday was nicer.

Somewhat, Jack added.

We had a reason for not being here, Phil said. A reason to stay in the city.

He's joined up now, Jack said.

The army? I asked.

The race, Jack answered. Posterity.

Oh? I said.

We're going to have a baby, Phil said. My wife and I. She is.

A new development, Jack said. A new twist.

Congratulations, I said.

Phil thanked me.

We just found out yesterday, he said. Just got the results.

Going to buy him a drink at the local bar, Jack said.

Where's your wife? I asked.

Stevie's sleeping, Phil said. She gets to sleep from now on, she says.

He laughed out loud.

She's a girl who loves her sleep, he said.

He seemed like a very nice guy; the elements had fallen together in him, the qualities combined in the right relations. He was sitting on top of the world now.

We've waited so long for this, he said.

It took about forty-five minutes to get to town. There wasn't all that much to recommend it once we did arrive, just a general store with a filling pump, a coffee shop, a bar. The people around had a naive look to them, a wide-eyed look, widely spaced features; inbred, I thought. I followed

Jack and Phil into the bar and was glad to be inside. It was
empty except for the bartender, a dark-haired man of
about fifty or so, very yellow teeth, tufts along his ears, and
an old man and a younger man sitting at the bar, smoking
Kents. It was very dark. We sat in wooden spindle-back
chairs at one of the round low tables. Jack went up to the
bar and brought back the first round.

Toast, Jack said, raising his glass.

To the new father, I said.

To the perpetuation of the flesh, Jack said.

We touched our glasses together.

Hear, hear, Phil said.

To Stevie, too, I offered.

Hear, hear, Jack said.

We touched our glasses again.

The difference of women, Jack announced.

I'll say, Phil said.

Miraculous, Jack said.

Absolutely, Phil said.

I'd almost given up thinking it was possible anymore,
Phil said. We thought, maybe it won't happen.

That's when it happens, Jack said. When you give up.

Thinking, I said.

Jack slapped me on the shoulder. He had big hands,
spatular hands.

That's it, he said.

Yeah, I said.

So why do you do it? he asked.

I made some sort of gesture with my hands, shrugging.

I can't stop, I said.

Stop what? Phil said.

He has a thinking problem, Jack said. It makes him ef-
feminate.

I was embarrassed by his remark, and stood up, saying I'd get the next round.

Good, Jack said. Good man.

At the bar I ordered three more beers. The bartender went about filling my request lackadaisically, hardly glancing down as he shoveled his hands into the cooler. The old man and his companion turned their heads and looked me over, and I thought I saw suspicion and mistrust in their eyes. But I had to remember it was dark. It wasn't good to assume. That may have been how they registered interest.

The beers were only seventy-five cents apiece. I left three dollars; the bartender flashed his yellow teeth at me. When I got back to the table Jack and Phil were deep into a discussion, as if I had never been there.

Not an easy process, Jack was saying. From beginning to end it is not an easy process.

The hardest part was trying, Phil said. We didn't seem to be getting anywhere and it was turning us bitter.

That happens, Jack said. You're accustomed to getting things, accustomed to producing. You see this all the time in business.

It came close, Phil said, very confidentially. The marriage, I mean. It really came close.

Crap, Jack said. You're still young.

Not that young, Phil said.

Young enough, Jack said.

If you want to know the truth, Phil said, lowering his voice even more. It wasn't like making love anymore.

I can understand that, I said.

Jack and Phil looked at me, and I had the sense of floating alone on a patch of ice.

I mean, I said. I've never tried to have a kid. But . . .

You married? Phil asked.

No, I said. I've been involved.

It's nearly the same, Phil said. But there's a difference. Take it from me.

When you're married, Jack said to me, you find out things about yourself you never knew were there. Dark things. Light things. You're not who you think you are.

You find that out a lot of ways, I said.

Not like marriage, Jack said. Marriage is forever. That's what does it to you: Forever.

Stevie wants a bigger house now, Phil said. All the way down here that's what she talked about. I kept saying, do we really need it?

Did she say yes? Jack asked.

She didn't say anything, Phil said. She didn't say yes or no. She just kept talking about a den, a playroom, a nursery.

Someplace quiet where you can do your own work, Jack said.

Someplace quiet where I can do my own work, Phil said.

Jack laughed.

It's an old story, he said.

He finished his beer. He was a fast drinker. Neither Phil nor I were half through.

I know it well, he said.

I'll get the next round, Phil said, starting to get up.

Jack put a hand on his arm.

No, I'll get it, he said.

But I want to get it, Phil said.

You can get the next round, Jack said. I'll get this one.

He got up from the table and made his way up to the bar, over which hung a cloud of smoke from the men who were sitting there smoking their Kents.

So you're not married, Phil said to me.

No, I said.

Lucky, he said. Sometimes I wish.

Do you? I asked.

Sometimes. Not very often.

He smiled. I smiled. I was jealous of him.

There can be days, he said, shaking his head. Oh boy, there can be days.

What do you do on those days? I asked.

Phil shrugged.

You get through, he said. You buy flowers. You learn the next time. You remember that raising your voice only gets you in the doghouse.

Who was it, I asked, that was always getting put in the doghouse? Some cartoon?

Some comic, Phil said. I don't remember.

I don't, either, I said. But I remember seeing it.

Me too, Phil said.

Jack came back with a tray of six beers, a bottle of whiskey, and three shot glasses.

I was just saying, Phil said, that there can be days even in the best couples. Would you say that's right?

I would say that's right and more, Jack said.

He sat down and passed around the bottle and the shot glasses.

Not your game though, is it? he said to me. You're more of the kiss 'em and make 'em cry type, aren't you? Kiss 'em and run.

What's that? Phil asked.

I heard it from a birdie, Jack said. A little birdie.

He opened up the bottle of whiskey and poured a shot for each of us. He raised his glass.

To the best of days, he said. To the days of light and promise.

We drank. The whiskey was hot going down my throat, melting things inside my chest.

Aah, Phil said.

When I got married, Jack said, I was doubtful about it being forever. I had my doubts, because of my expectations.

Right, Phil said. You're right.

My expectations were forever as an instant thing, Jack said. A thing I would know instantly.

But you have to wait, Phil said.

He poured another round of shots.

Not only do you have to wait, Jack said, but what you wait for is contrary to your expectations.

We drank the second round of shots.

Sometimes I hate my wife, Jack said. Sometimes she is everything I never wanted.

It was after four when we left the bar. The sky was dark gray. Rain was imminent; the expectation of it hung in the air. Yet we didn't hurry. The other two were better men than I, stock upright, carrying their liquor. I was having a hard time. It seemed to me vitally important to maintain a clear, constant contact with a voice above and slightly to the left of my right temple. *A little to the left, a little to the right. Lift your knee now. Breathe.* I wanted to throw up, to pitch the fiery contents of my insides, but the voice said no.

When we got to the rise which led down to the cabins, we stopped. Jack turned to me and said, I'm going to give you a piece of advice.

Okay, I said.

He squinted.

You're an asshole, he said. You're shit.

I shot a glance at Phil. He looked away.

Thanks, I said. Thank you, Jack.

I pushed my hands into the shorts pockets and tried to stand straight.

You think you're smart, he said. Playing your hand very close to your chest. But it's not smart. It's shitless. That's what you are. Shitless.

Asshole to shit to shitless in less than a minute, that's impressive, I said. Thanks, Jack.

See what I mean? Jack asked. Thanks, Jack. Why don't you say Jack, fuck off? Jack, who the fuck do you think you are, standing on the side of the road, you miserable old wash-up? Why don't you respond?

Jack, fuck off, I said.

He started to weave a little bit. A look passed over his face.

Good, he said, though. Better.

Who the fuck do you think you are? I said.

He leaned in, patting my face heavily.

Good, he said. But you want to know something?

What? I asked.

I know about you, he said. I do.

He backed away from me, and started down the hill towards the cabins. The heat and the haze crouched down all around me, pressing down. I squatted a little, bending my knees, taking deep breaths that didn't help much. The only relief would be to get out of the heat and lay down somewhere in private. Phil took me by the arm.

I wouldn't take it to heart, he said.

I don't, I said, between breaths. I think it's funny.

That's it, Phil said. That's the way.

There was a halfhearted volleyball game going on when we got back to the cabin: Andrew, George, Heidi, and Sam on

one team; Mickey, Paul, Robb, and Tina on the other. Kate
stood on the sidelines and snapped pictures. The youngest
child, Melissa, was sitting on the steps with a dark-haired
woman, who I figured was Stevie Hazlett.

It still hadn't started to rain, but I could smell it now; the
air was thickening, gathering mass.

Woo-oo, Heidi called as we rounded the corner of the
house. We're winning!

Not yet, Mickey said.

Phil went over to sit down on the steps with his wife. He
leaned over and kissed her over Melissa's head; Stevie
made a face and laughed and fanned the air around her
nose, and told him that he smelled like a brewery.

Jack went to stand next to Kate, and she turned on him
with the camera and took a couple of quick pictures, then
bent down to change her film. I could see him looking down
at the bare nape of her neck. He reached his fingers down
towards her. I wondered what he must be thinking, touching her right out in the open like that. Heidi glanced over at
them, and he took a step away.

Come join us, honey, Heidi said.

Jack shook his head, belched, and laughed. Heidi
wagged her hand and laughed. She was nervous; it was in
her face.

Oh you, she said.

I'm out of film, Kate said to Jack.

She stood up.

There's a box in the cellar, she said. I don't think it's
really good. But we can see.

She took off through the side door into the cellar. Jack
walked off after her. Heidi let the ball fly past her face. She
turned to Sam.

Go help your daddy, she said.

Okay! he said.

He went running after Jack, into the basement.

Daddydaddydaddydaddy! he shouted.

That boy loves his father, Heidi said, to anybody and everybody.

Hey, lazy, Paul shouted to me. We need a player now.

Not me, I said.

I staggered towards the steps. I didn't want to be around when Kate and Jack came out from the cellar. That was one thing I could spare myself. Stevie and Phil shifted to let me pass and I nodded to them.

Way to go, I said to Stevie.

She looked at me, confused and not very warm.

I mean, congratulations, I said.

Oh, she said. Thanks.

She had little lines around her mouth, tight lines. She was pretty, though. They were a handsome couple, as Heidi had said.

I went inside and upstairs, pausing in the bathroom to make sure I wasn't going to throw up. I drank a few glasses of water, which I remembered was a good thing to do, and then keeping my hand against the wall I slid towards my bedroom and flopped belly down on top of the covers, kicking off my sneakers and burying my face in the pillow. I felt hot and feverish. The room didn't spin, but it wobbled a little, and I couldn't feel my bones. They seemed all to be in separate pieces strewn across the bed, my insides running across and over them, spilling over. Then there was darkness, and only the sound of grown-up voices, playing.

I woke up once, and the room was much darker; the sun must have set. Andrew was sitting on my side of the bed, his hands underneath my shirt, pressing his fingers into the muscles of my back.

Why are you doing that? I mumbled.

To be nice, he said. Just to be nice.

He continued on for a little while.

Why? I asked at length. Why are you being nice?

I don't know, Andrew said. It feels good.

I wish you wouldn't, I said.

Why? he said.

His voice seemed to come from very far away.

Because I'm not in love with you, I said.

Did I ask you to be? he said.

No, I said.

Is that what you think I want? he said.

I pondered that for a while. *It's what I would want*, I thought.

What do you think? he said.

I think that's what you want, I said. I think so.

That's not what I want, he said.

What do you want then? I asked.

Just to be nice, he said.

I don't believe that, I said. I don't believe that at all.

He pulled his hands out from under my shirt, smoothing the back of it.

That's too bad, he said. I feel very sorry for you, then.

Don't bother, I said. I have sorry enough.

I came up again, reluctantly, when Kate rubbed the palm of her hand flat on my back, shaking back and forth.

Old bear, she was saying. Old man. Wake up.

I opened my eyes. In the darkness I could just make out her face, bending into mine. I turned over on my back, groaning.

Good boy, she said. Take something nice.

She lifted my head in the crook of her arm and with her free hand tilted a glass of water against my lips.

Drink, she said. It will give you courage and strength. Take away the horrors.

I sipped a few sips. She pressed the glass higher and made me take gulps. Some of it spilled out the corners of my mouth, down my chin, and onto my chest.

Good boy, she said. Good man. Can you sit up?

I nodded a little and she helped, lifting my head in her arm, taking some of my weight.

Silly old man, she said, when I was positioned leaning against the wall, blinking my eyes open and shut.

Her face started coming clearer in the dark.

Going out in the middle of the day, she said. Do you feel better now?

I nodded again and pressed my head against the wall.

Except for my entire body, I said.

We sent Andrew up to make you feel better, Kate said. But he came down looking very pale. Were you a mean old bear to him? Did you make him feel bad?

I told him I didn't love him, I told her.

That wasn't very nice, she said.

It was the truth, I said.

What's the truth? she said. Only straw. Only dead leaves. Mean old bear.

Scared bear, I said. The bear is scared.

Scared of what? Kate asked.

I shook my head.

The dark? she asked.

Maybe, I said.

Maybe he likes the dark. This bear. Maybe he loves the dark too well.

Maybe.

Maybe he loves it and he's scared of it.

Maybe.

Poor bear.

I made room for her on the bed and she leaned against the wall next to me, her head against my ear. I could smell the sweat on her; it mixed with my own. She held my hand. We could hear voices downstairs, people laughing and talking, gathering together, mixing things to drink.

Why don't you leave me alone? I asked. Please leave me alone.

I will, Kate said. I'm going to do something tonight.

She lit her cigarette and blew out the match. The sulfur smell was strong under my nose.

But now that I've told you, she whispered, you're guilty along with me. Help me.

A moment passed, while I absorbed her remark.

What do you want? I asked her.

Talk to Heidi, she told me. Keep her occupied.

No, I said.

I want your blessing, she whispered.

No, I said. Not for this. No.

It's not her, Kate said. It has nothing to do with her.

I know, I said.

She squeezed my hand, hard, digging her nails into my palm. We were alike. The same night was in both of us, the same pitch, the same tangle of desires.

It's bigger than that, she said.

I know, I said.

Help, she said.

I couldn't see her face. She'd turned away from me and was looking towards the door, where all the voices came through from downstairs. Last winter I'd told her I loved her; she said if she could love anyone it would be me. *You love Paul,* I said. *Yes,* she said, *I do love Paul. Well? You don't love me,* she said, *not me, but something else.*

I won't help you, I said.

You know how to hurt a girl, she said.

I know, I said. It's a gift.

PART THREE

9

DOWNSTAIRS IN THE LIVING ROOM, the kids were playing Chutes and Ladders with Robb. Heidi was sitting on the sofa with Andrew, and they both had sandwiches and paper plates on their laps, with potato chips and pickles. Robb had an open beer at his side. His face was flushed. He was either drunk or well on his way.

There's cold cuts in the kitchen, Heidi told me.

I don't think I can eat, I said.

I wish it would hurry up and rain, Heidi said. This waiting is killing me.

Andrew wiped a crumb off the side of his face.

Aren't you going to eat anything? he asked me.

No, I said. I don't think so.

I find it so hard to eat when it's humid, Heidi said. I have to force myself.

I never have a problem eating, Andrew said.

Well, you're so skinny, Heidi said.

I watched the game for a little while. Robb let Sam get ahead of him, and Sam was happy, throwing the dice and clapping his hands. Tina looked impatient. Robb asked her to go into the kitchen and get him another beer. She said no, and Heidi told her not to be rude. Tina shot an ugly look at her mother, then left.

I went out the screen door onto the porch. Everyone else

was out there. Stevie and Phil Hazlett were leaning against each other with their backs against the porch railing; Phil had his arm around his wife. George and Paul were sitting at the wrought-iron table in the corner. Kate and Jack were sitting in two folding chairs, facing out towards the lake, hardly moving. Their stillness seemed to have an element of uneasiness in it. Mickey was sitting on the steps. There was a glimmer of lightning from far away, but no sound of thunder.

It's been doing that for a while now, Paul told me.

Have a beer, Jack said.

No thanks, I said.

I sat on the railing, in the corner, so I could see everybody, and with just a little turn of the head, I could also see the whole outdoors. It was interesting, looking at people's faces in the dark: Faces are so beautiful when only the essential lines show.

I have a memory of my mother, Kate said. How she would sit on the front stoop of our house and watch the rain come down. She could do that for hours.

I don't remember that, Paul said.

You wouldn't, Kate replied. You were scared of rain.

Rain is mysterious, Stevie said.

She told me thunder was the devil laughing, Kate said.

How horrible, Stevie said.

Depends on how you feel about the devil, Jack said.

You can't go in the water when there's lightning, can you? Kate asked.

Or under trees, Stevie said.

From where I sat I could only see Kate's profile, only half the story. We had left things at a stalemate. I told her I thought what she was going to do was pointless; pointless and stupid. She told me I could go further and I would not be wrong. I asked her if it was some roundabout way of getting back at me for abandoning her the way I did, and she said, on the contrary, she was paving the way for my release.

Did you read about the family? George said across the porch to Stevie.

In Brooklyn? she asked.

Was it Brooklyn? Mickey said. I thought it was the Bronx.

One or the other, Stevie said.

Awful, George said.

Was it all of them? Stevie asked.

Oh yes, George said, taking off his glasses and wiping them, though why he needed to in the dark was a mystery.

I don't think all of them, Phil said.

I hope not, Stevie said.

No, it was all of them, George said. I'm sure. Can you imagine? One minute you're having lunch . . .

It's too horrible, Stevie said. It is. Too horrible.

There was just the basket left, Mickey said. All over the front page there was that picture of just the picnic basket left, sitting under the trees.

Can you imagine? George repeated. An entire family burned to death by lightning?

I had thought, when it happened, that all the attention around the story was morbid. Waiting for the rain now, I wondered if all the publicity was less a sign of fear than of some deep need to know that at any moment our burdens could be lifted. Suddenly, in a kiss of grace, all problems could be wiped away.

It's really terrible, Stevie said.

Somebody did survive, Phil said. Two people. I'm sure.

It *is* terrible, George said.

Two of them survived, Phil insisted.

All right, George said. Maybe you're right.

I'll have a beer now, I said.

I thought you weren't coming back to us, Paul said.

No, I said. I'm back.

George reached down into the cooler that was by his feet and tossed me a can of beer. Afterwards he rubbed his side, as if he had a stitch. Mickey saw it and asked him if he was all right, and he nodded and said he was.

Sam came running to the screen door and pressed his face against the mesh.

I won, Daddy! he yelled. I won!

Put your shoes on if you're going outside, Heidi shouted. Put your flip-flops on.

Let's play another game, Robb called.

I won, Daddy, Sam said, trying to press his face through the screen.

Good for you, son, Jack said.

Come play with me, Sam said.

Leave your father alone, Heidi called.

Let's play another game, Sam, said Robb.

Play with your sisters, Heidi said. Leave Daddy alone.

Come on, Sam, Robb insisted, slurring the words slightly. A championship round.

Daddy, Sam said.

Leave Daddy alone, Heidi said.

Daddy, Sam repeated.

There was a glimmer of lightning in the sky over the lake, bluish-white.

Better close the windows on the cabin, Jack said.

Are you going to go close the windows? Heidi called.

Jack didn't answer. We heard Robb ask Tina to be a good girl and get him another beer.

Would you pick up their pajamas if you go over? Heidi asked Jack. I can change them over here. Do you mind if I change them over here, neighbors?

No, Mickey answered.

Nope, Robb said.

They're cranky, Heidi said. Sam's getting cranky.

What time is it? I asked.

Quarter to ten, Mickey said. You were out, all right.

I should eat something, probably, I said.

Jack got up from his chair and started for the stairs. The porch floor squeaked under his weight.

There's a chocolate cake, Jack, Heidi said. You might as well bring that back, too. And more beer.

I've got two hands, Heidi, Jack said.

You can carry it, Heidi said.

I'll go, Kate said. I'll help.

He can carry it, Heidi said. He's a big boy.

Daddy, Sam sang. Daddy Daddy Daddy Daddy.

For Pete's sake, Sam! Heidi snapped. Leave your father alone.

They're cute when they're that age aren't they? Phil said.

When they behave, Stevie muttered.

Ours will behave, Phil said.

The beer is in the back of the refrigerator, Heidi called. The cake is in a plastic in the cupboard.

I'll help, Kate said.

Mickey shifted, as she and Jack went down the stairs. Kate did not look at me again. I was suddenly conscious of how thick the night was, as if I'd just landed in it. Kate and Jack disappeared into the woods, lit once by a glimmer in the sky.

Above the sink, Heidi shouted to Jack from the living room. It's in the cupboard above the sink.

Smell the ozone? Mickey said. It's going to rain soon. It's really going to rain.

I hope so, George said. I don't think I can wait anymore.

Kate? Heidi called. Did Kate go with him?

Rumblings of thunder could be heard getting closer. There was a restless, tingly feeling in the air. Stevie wanted to go home before the storm hit, but Phil didn't; he was talking with George. Stevie went into a pout. The tense lines around her mouth got deeper, and she wouldn't enter into the conversation. I could feel how she wanted to make everyone uncomfortable.

I went into the kitchen. Paul followed and sat on the table, watching while I dug some ham and lettuce and mustard out of the refrigerator.

Well, it's a night, he said.

I guess so, I replied.

It upsets you, doesn't it, he said. Her going off.

No, I said. Not at all.

I'll bet, he said.

I brought the sandwich things to the table and started putting things together. Paul bumped his leg against my knee, being very much himself: Some people are very much themselves, and I do my best to avoid them, because I know that I can become very possessive. I want that quality in them, whatever it is. My father was possessive. It drove him crazy because he wanted to have my mother as much as he wanted God. I don't know why my mother stayed with him, under that kind of pressure all the time. I asked her once; she said it was her duty. I thought that was a stupid, shallow reason. From that time, any strong or deep feeling I had for her started to collapse. If she thought of herself no better than that, I wouldn't, either.

Do you love your sister? I asked Paul.

That's a dumb question, he replied.

Do you? I asked.

She's my sister, he said.

That's not yes, I said.

There was a tremendous bang, like an explosion. The kids in the living room screamed and I jumped a little, too. The rain started to pour down, heaving. Paul bumped his knee against my leg again and I pushed it away.

Keep yourself to yourself, I told him.

Prude, he said. Prudish.

No, I said. I know what I don't want.

He hopped off the table.

Preacher's son, he said. That's what it is. Pious prude.

If you love your sister, I told him, you're a bastard to stay around. And if you don't, you're a bastard, too.

We do what we can, she and I, Paul said. The best we can.

Maybe that's not good enough sometimes, I said.

Maybe not, he said. It's still the best we can.

Well, I said.

You're self-righteous, he said. That's you. You're the one who makes her unhappy. You're the one who shouldn't stick around.

He left the room, and I stood at the table and tried to eat my sandwich. I didn't get past more than a few bites. I threw away what was left.

In the living room, Chutes and Ladders lay abandoned in the middle of the floor, playing pieces scattered in all directions. Everyone had gone out on the front porch to watch the rain, and I went to the screen door to look, too, as great cracks of brilliant blue slashed the air, lighting everything harshly. The clearing, lake and dock looked like a stage set when the lightning flashed, very artfully put together, very detailed; but imitation. Maybe it was the cold paleness of the light. Things took on reality again in the dark, in the pauses between strikes, in the dimness where edges weren't distinct. *They'd be in the thick of it right now.*

I looked at Heidi standing very close to the wall of the house next to the door, her three kids huddled very near. She had her arms around Sam's and Tina's shoulders. *Ladybug, ladybug, fly away home.* I hated knowing secrets, knowing the score. What would be the more grievous error — to say something, or not? There are no bystanders who do not approve.

Where's Kate? Robb asked, in such a low voice that nobody else seemed to have heard him; at any rate, no one answered. The lightning played and the rain came down.

Wonders in heaven above and signs in the earth below, Paul quoted.

Where's Kate? Robb asked again, more loudly.

She went to help Jack, Mickey said.

Oh, Robb said.

Sam started to cry, wanting his father, and Andrew tried to get him to go back inside, saying they'd play a nice game of Chutes and Ladders. I could see Stevie start to get annoyed. She got tense around the jaw and I thought, *Get used to it — kids are sweet until they're a pain. They have a sixth sense for weak moments.* Paul told Sam a story about a little boy who became the rain.

You'd think they'd come back, Heidi murmured.

It's coming down hard, I said.

Still, she said, you'd think they'd try. I want the kids to have a wash. They're sweaty. I don't want to put them back in sweaty clothes.

Mommy, I want cake, Tina said.

George wondered aloud if the rain would kill many of the fish in the lake, and he and Phil started in about toxins and dioxins, denser molecules hanging in the air, coming down in the rain. They sounded as if they enjoyed it.

Mommy, cake, Tina whined again.

Paul put his arm around her.

There's another story, he said. About a girl who turned into cake.

You'd think they'd goddamn come back, Heidi said.

Nobody turns into cake, Tina said.

They need a bath, dammit, Heidi said.

I volunteered to help give the two younger kids a bath. I had a sense that she'd be willing to go if she didn't have to go alone, if she had someone to talk to. She was very efficient, actually. I didn't help so much as just talk with her. She could do many things at once without concentrating on any of them — scrub the kids and run a glass of water and drink a beer and have a conversation. She could spread herself without getting thin. I didn't even talk, so much as listen.

A homosexual man in the bathroom with my children naked, she said. My sister would croak, being born again. Which to my mind is a real pity, since the first time was already a mistake . . . She tells me this thing going around is a condemnation from God. What George has. I tell her I don't know what to think.

Is George sick? I asked.

Me and my mouth, Heidi said. You're probably not supposed to know.

I won't say anything, I said.

Thanks, she said.

She picked around among all the shampoo bottles along the tub ledge, picking them up and setting them down, in turn. None of them seemed to satisfy her.

I guess there wouldn't be any baby shampoo, she said finally. I like to use that no-more-tears lather. Oh, well.

She picked an expensive-looking bottle with a streamlined logo and complicated ingredients. Pouring some into her palm, she started rubbing it on Sam's head. Sam squeezed his eyes shut and bared his teeth, making a sound like car brakes squealing. While she worked on Sam's hair, she asked me if I was the woman or the man in a relationship. I was shocked at first, then I told her that it wasn't that easy, it didn't fall into neat areas like that.

No, I guess it wouldn't, she said. I kissed a girl once. It was weird. Just fooling around. It was like kissing myself.

I recognize that, I said.

Like Jack, she said, lowering her voice. Jack won't kiss me after certain acts, because he says it would be like doing it to himself.

She rinsed Sam's hair, and turned to shampoo Melissa, who got soap in her eyes and started to cry. Heidi had to spend a little time calming her down and rinsing her eyes. Sam started having sympathy pains. I distracted him with a soap bar submarine.

Who knows anymore? Heidi said when things were calm again. Almost everything you hear anymore is a crock. I have an aunt who says everything is because of moon rocks. Everything's going to the dogs because the astronauts took rocks off the moon where they belonged, and brought them back here, where they don't belong.

I hadn't heard that, I said.

Yeah, Heidi said. Nobody has. She's the only one.

We should introduce her to Andrew, I said.

Andrew? she asked, her expression blank.

Skinny Andrew, I said. Downstairs.

Oh right, she said. For a minute I forgot.

He believes in things from outer space too, I said.

You know, Heidi said, I heard somewhere that the moon landing never really happened. On the moon, that is. They say it really happened somewhere out in Arizona or Nevada. The whole thing was just a fake.

They say a lot of things, I said.

But it's one of the most monumental things, she said. I remember my dad running to get the camera to take a picture of it on TV.

I nodded.

They also say that Kennedy isn't dead, she said. That he's off in Alaska somewhere — with Marilyn Monroe.

Collecting moon rocks, I said.

She smiled.

No, she said. But they say, too, that Judy Garland isn't dead. And Clark Gable. And that Watergate was covering up something else. And that nobody asked us to go in Vietnam. And that we knew about Pearl Harbor before it was going to happen. All these things . . . all these things that we're supposed to believe, and now who knows what we're supposed to believe anymore. I mean, Walt Disney is sitting around somewhere, all frozen, waiting for a cure for cancer so he can come back to life. It's strange.

She turned on the tap to warm up the water in the tub a little before going on.

She continued, I said to Jack, *I want to stay in Jersey*. I want to be able to bring my kids up in a place that's pleasant and safe. I don't want them getting mixed up in a lot of crazy shit. But it's hard to get away from all of it. It's either moon rocks or it's something else.

Some places are better than others, I said. They're less confusing.

My parents bent over backwards to make sure we had all the things they never had, she said. They wanted us to be happy. They wanted us to be secure. But it seems to me now that they were doing it for themselves more than for us. I see it with my own kids. I buy them toys, I buy them clothes, we got this cabin in the woods — all supposedly for them, so they would have. But I go to sleep wondering all the time if I'm not just giving them things because I don't know what else to do. I don't know really what to give them. There's so much crazy stuff happening out there, and every day it comes from someplace different. Every day there's something else I didn't think about, someone else I thought I could trust. And I'm afraid that someday I'll wake up, and it'll be me.

There was a knock on the door, and Tina pushed her head in from the hall. She stood in the frame pressing her head against the door and holding the knob with both hands.

Mommy, she said, I'm tired.

I know, Heidi said. We're going home as soon as I dry the little ones.

Do you have to? I said.

Heidi looked at me point-blank.

They have to get dry, she said.

Go home, I mean. In the middle of the rain.

Tina swung back and forth on the door handle. She threw me a sour look, then concentrated on her mother, willing her to make something happen, to make the rain stop, make them all be home in a twinkling of an eye.

You're going to break that door if you don't stop that,

Heidi told her. And then Mommy and Daddy will have to pay for it and we will never be invited here again.

I want to go home, Tina said.

In a minute, Heidi said.

She pulled the plug out of the tub. The water started to go down.

I mean *home* home, Tina said. I miss home.

Good grief, Tina, Heidi said.

She bent over and lifted Sam from the tub, and started to dry him off. Water dripped off his body onto the floor, making a puddle that channeled through the grooves where the tiles didn't meet. Melissa splashed at the receding water in the tub, slapping the surface with the palms of both hands. Sam yawned, eyes closed, mouth open wide.

It galls me sometimes, Heidi said.

Sam started patting her face and accidentally stuck his finger in her eye.

Damn you, she said to him, smacking his hand. Now stay still.

Are you all right? I asked her.

Do you ever go through this? she asked me. Do you go through this being left to do everything by yourself? It just galls me sometimes.

Actually, I said, I never stay around long enough.

That's why they call it gay, she said. That's got to be it.

I bet you're right, I said.

She asked me to finish drying Sam. I worked the towel over him, trying to be careful, though I wasn't really sure what careful was. Heidi lifted Melissa out and started to dry her.

What should we say to Daddy when we get home? Heidi asked the kids. Should we make him sleep in the car?

They didn't say anything. More than anything they were just tired.

Should we tell him the car? Heidi asked.

Tina started swinging on the door handle again.

I told you to stop that, Heidi said.

I reached behind me and grabbed the pile of Sam's things, his miniature undershorts, little short pants, and tiny T-shirt. *Such detailed expressions*, I thought. They seemed somehow thoughtful. Sam leaned his hands on my shoulders as I knelt down on the wet floor and helped him on with his things. He pushed his face close to mine and started barking, slamming his little hands against my shoulders over and over. Saliva start running down his chin, and he laughed as I half closed my eyes.

Get your clothes on, Sam, Heidi said.

Get your clothes on, Sam, he repeated.

Don't talk back, Heidi said.

Are we going home now? Tina asked.

In a minute, Heidi said.

She started dressing Melissa.

Why don't you wait? I said.

I hate putting sweaty clothes on them, she said, more to herself than to me. Come on, Tina. We're going, Sam.

She finished with Melissa and stood up. Sam threw himself at my chest, clinging like a monkey.

Come on, Sam, Heidi said. We're going.

No! Sam said.

He wouldn't let go of me, and to make things easier I carried him downstairs that way, hanging against my chest. Heidi came behind me and Tina came trailing after, head down, creeping. We went out to the porch. It was still coming down heavily. Heidi stood staring out at it, holding Melissa on one hip, while Tina clung to her other leg.

You're not going home in this, Mickey said.

We have to go home, Heidi said. The kids are tired. I'm tired. We have to go.

There was a huge crash of thunder, a ripping sound. Tina screamed and Sam pushed his face into my chest.

You are *not* going home in this, Mickey said.

Sam started whining for his father.

Oh, Jesus God, Heidi said.

10

W*E ALL TRIED* to convince Heidi to stay; she gave in when we gave her permission to go if the rain slacked off, even a little bit. She wasn't happy, but she gave in. Only Robb didn't join in; he sat at the table staring at his beer. But when Heidi decided, he looked up and grinned at her.

Good show, he said, slurring.

Everybody laughed.

My brother the lush, Mickey said, and everybody laughed again, and relaxed a little.

Mickey took the kids into the kitchen and found some chocolate powder in one of the cupboards. He mixed some chocolate milk for them, which pacified them a bit; they were quiet when they came back out from the kitchen.

I watched Heidi sitting in the chair Jack had been in, chewing the side of her mouth, trying to relax, trying to get down a few sips of beer. She had Melissa on her lap. Tina and Sam sat next to her on the floor. George had moved from the table to where Mickey now sat, leaning against the wall. Their shoulders touched. The rain came down, while thunder and lightning chased each other in the night sky.

Is this a hurricane? Melissa asked her mother.

No, honey, Heidi said. This is just rain.

Is there deadness in it? Melissa said.

What did she say? Stevie asked.

We heard about hurricanes on the TV, Heidi explained. How many deaths, and so on. We have a curiosity about that because the C-A-T recently D-I-E-D.

The cat died, Tina said, bored.

Heidi slapped her on the arm.

Thank you very much, she said.

The cat is dead, Melissa said.

Now you've got her started, Heidi said. Thank you very much.

Tina moved away to stand by the table where Paul and Robb were. Robb looked up from his beer. He started whistling softly.

We are fascinated with deadness now, Heidi explained to Stevie. We want to know what deadness is. We wanted to dig up the cat and look at its deadness.

Oh boy, Tina said.

I really want her to forget about it, Heidi said. I don't want her to start getting scared.

I think we could stop on this subject now, Mickey said.

George patted his arm.

It's all right, he said.

There was a crash of thunder almost simultaneous with a burst of lightning that lit up the whole surface of the lake. The storm was right overhead, now, and the wind was strong. We all got a little damp, as the rain blew onto the porch. It felt good.

Is there deadness in rain? Melissa asked.

No, honey, Heidi said. There's only rain in rain.

Cute, Phil said to his wife.

While the rest of the party relaxed, Heidi got more tense. I watched her in the half light of the storm, wondering if it was because she knew, or because she didn't know. Either way, it came down to the same thing, so I started to drink methodically. Whatever I did now would come down to the same thing. There was no choice at all.

I started to laugh.

At the table, Robb pointed his finger at me.

You're part of it, he said. Goddamn part of it.

What? somebody said; I didn't know who.

Shut up, Robb, Mickey said.

You know what's going on, Robb said. You know what's goddamn going on. You know what's what.

Robb, Mickey repeated.

Robb stood up. Paul tried to grab his arm, but he swung himself away, and in doing so, he lost his balance and knocked into Tina. She started to cry. Robb bent to apologize to her, which only made it worse; she started shrieking, putting on a big show. Heidi had to put Melissa down and gather Tina onto her lap. Robb stood there mumbling how sorry he was, but nobody paid attention. Heidi stroked Tina's back, rhythmically, saying, *There, there,* and pretty soon she stopped crying. Heidi held her close and kissed her cheek.

She looked around for the other two kids: Melissa was sitting with Stevie Hazlett.

Where's Sam? she asked.

He went inside about ten minutes ago, Mickey said.

No, it was more than that, Stevie said.

Sam? Heidi called.

I thought he was going to the bathroom, Mickey said. Maybe he's lying down.

Sam? Heidi called, again, a little louder.

I'll look for him, Andrew said.

He went into the house, banging the screen door behind

him. We could hear him calling Sam's name every now and then. Then it was quiet for a while. Another peal of thunder sounded, not quite so loud, and the lightning didn't follow right away. The storm was passing away from us. We heard Andrew calling for Sam again. Heidi got up to go into the house but Tina didn't want to let her go.

Oh Tina, she said, exasperation in her voice. Stop whining.

She pushed the girl away and went into the house.

Sam? she called. Sam, goddamn you.

Andrew came to the screen door and said he couldn't find the boy. Except for George and Robb, everybody stood up, listening as Heidi called Sam's name. A few minutes later she came to the door.

I can't find him, she said. He's gone after his father. He must have gone looking for his father.

Does he know where the cabin is? Mickey asked.

He's four years old, Heidi said.

She started to cry.

He's only four years old, she said.

Mickey went into the house to get a flashlight. Phil Hazlett ran down the back steps and into the rain, and Paul followed him. I went into the house with Stevie and Andrew, and together, Heidi, Andrew, and I went out front to look. George stayed with the two girls.

It was messy work. Though the rain was just starting to die down, it got in our eyes, and the ground was slippery under our feet. Twice I almost slipped in the mud. We searched the trees for Sam. Heidi was the first to see Jack and Kate coming towards us. They had Sam, safe, between them. All three were soaked to the skin.

Heidi ran up to Jack and started screaming at him, asking where the hell had he been, and why hadn't he come back with the kids' pajamas and the cake like he was supposed to, and who the hell did he think he was and what the hell did he think he was doing? Jack took it for a while and then cut her short, saying she was supposed to have been watching the kids, and if anything had happened it would have been her own goddamn fault. Heidi stood still for a minute, her mouth hanging open, her hair wet and sticking to her head. Then she slapped Jack across the face.

Kate took a step back, taking Sam with her. The goofy, slack smile spread over Jack's face. He swung his arm and caught Heidi on the side of her head so hard that she fell. Or maybe he didn't hit her that hard; maybe she slipped on the mud. But she sat on the ground and started to scream, which brought the others running.

I wish they had come faster. Even though I was sure that if I did something it would be worse, it was also true that if I didn't do anything, it would be just as bad. It came down to the same damn thing. And the crux tore at me.

It took three of the men to pull Jack off of me, and by the time they managed to do so, there was blood running down my mouth and down my face, mixing with the rain. I was already thinking it had been a stupid thing to do, to run at him as I had, swinging: Jack was trained in the use of his hands and I was not. But I had lost control of myself. I couldn't stop myself, so now I was on the ground, covered with mud and clutching my stomach. Everything hurt.

Robb staggered over to Kate, trying to keep his balance on the wet ground. He stared at her for a long time.

You're a bitch, he said sadly. You're just a bitch.

Kate stared back, the rain dripping off her face, plastering down her short hair. I wanted to tell Robb, *You're right,* but I couldn't speak; I couldn't find my voice. I wanted to tell him he was missing something.

No doubt about it, Robb-O, Kate said. That's what I am.

Robb stood dumbly, having pulled the right answer out of the wrong hat, having missed an element which I'd found: Whether you struggled or not, whether you tried or not, it ended up the same way with people — hurting them, making them unhappy. Kate didn't try to make people happy. Neither did I. But I had put a lot of effort into not trying.

Andrew and Paul helped Heidi up from the ground, and walked her inside. George took hold of Sam. Mickey grabbed for me, but I fought him off. I wanted to stay where I was.

Jack and Phil stood arguing some paces away. Jack wanted to go into the house after Heidi, and Phil was telling him that the best thing right now would be to stay away. Jack said *no, no, no.* Their voices faded in and out of the rain.

Kate bent down in front of me and touched my face.

Don't, I said. Go away.

She pulled her hand away. I didn't look up and I didn't hear her leave, though she must have.

Jack took off into the trees, yelling, and Phil ran after, shouting his name.

I curled myself into a ball and let the rain soak me through.

Some time later, Paul and Andrew finally came out and carried me into the house. I only put up a little bit of a fight, because I was getting tired and cold. Anyway, sooner or later it would stop raining and get light. Sooner or later the next day would come.

Everyone tried to be nice. Paul said my bruises looked pretty, but Mickey said, no, purple was not my color. Andrew rubbed my feet, the only part of me that didn't hurt. I didn't stop him. I figured, what the hell at this point: It wouldn't make any difference now. Except for the physical pain, I was quite content.

Mickey went into the kitchen to make hot toddies for me and for George, who was sitting across from me, shivering in a chair. He shouldn't have gone out into the rain. Heidi was upstairs with the kids and Stevie Hazlett was looking after them. They had all stopped crying by the time I came in. The house was pretty quiet. I didn't know where Robb had gone, and I didn't ask.

The rain still came down, though more lightly. Mickey finally took George upstairs to bed; a little while later he came down with a towel and wrapped it around my shoulders, so I would start getting dry. I think they might all have felt more comfortable if I'd said something, and I would have been happy to, except the only thing I could think to say was that things being the way they were, I'd been a dope to try to make them otherwise. But it wouldn't have come out right, because my face was all mashed up; so I didn't say anything.

It was Andrew who finally suggested that maybe the best thing would be to leave me alone. I mumbled that I would be very grateful, and he smiled and said it was okay. They left me with my hot drink, which stung as it went down; but after a few sips I didn't mind as much. I couldn't smoke, though, because my lips were puffy and raw. I thought about Sam, wondering whether he would remember this night, and if he did, whether he would spend his life, too, looking for ways to hold himself back, trying to make things otherwise. I wondered if he would try to keep everything from sliding down into the same damn thing.

The rain stopped just before dawn. For a few minutes there was complete silence. Then the birds started. As I sat listening to them, I noticed some strange calls; familiar, but out of place. I dragged myself off the sofa and across the room to see what was up. I couldn't make out anything through the screen door so I went out onto the porch, but the roof blocked most of the sky. I ended up having to go down the steps and into the yard. There was a lot of mud, and the grass was very wet.

I saw Kate standing at the far end of the dock. Her back was to me. Above her swirled as many as a dozen sea gulls, possibly more, crying in their strange voices. They had come inland, at least ten miles, and were circling and diving over the lake. I walked across the yard towards them. Kate turned around when she heard me step onto the dock.

You look awful, she said.

I feel fine, I said. Peachy.

I feel terrible, she said.

You look fine, I said.

We watched each other for a while, hardly blinking.

I'm sorry you got all bloody over what I did, Kate said.

It wasn't over you, I told her. It had nothing to do with you.

Not even a little? she asked.

All right, I said. A little.

If I hadn't done what I did, she began.

If wishes were horses, I said.

She looked smaller than I'd ever seen her, tighter; she was all wet. The gulls swooped and dove all around her, their cries triumphant and rude, and I saw what had brought them so far inland. I looked back at Kate. It started to get lighter out; across the lake, the top of the sun came over the hill.

My father used to hit my mother, I said. He used to hit her and then go talk about God.

Kate closed her eyes.

It wasn't just once, I said. It was all the time. In front of other people, even. Nobody said anything. Can you imagine? My mother made excuses for him. Why didn't I say something?

Kate opened her eyes.

Stupid, she said, thinking you could do something about it now.

That's a good one, I said.

I walked out next to her. We watched the sea gulls diving for dead fish bellied up in the water. Insects swarmed around the bodies closer to the dock. A live fish, jumping to catch some in its mouth, was wrenched up in the jaws of a swooping gull. The sun rose red over the hill. The birds sang louder, and the sound they made was almost unbearable.

You want to hear something else good? I said. I worked so hard to keep it from happening in me. And because I worked so hard . . .

Yes, that's good, Kate said.

It might have been you, I said.

You stayed away.

What else could I do?

Nothing, she said. Obviously.

She pointed to the swirling gulls.

Listen, she said. Listen to them call each other.

I looked up. They rose so high. I pictured myself as they

might see me — small, painfully small, so small it was funny — and I heard laughter, sounds of pure delight.

You think they're calling each other? I asked.

Kate sighed. No, she said.

What do you think then?

I don't know, she said. Maybe.

I slid my arm around her waist, and she leaned her head against my shoulder. The sky grew brighter.

Yes, she said.

I'm glad, I said. I'm glad.

Her whole body started shaking, and I pressed her close. After a little while her shaking stopped. We stood still, watching the day break.

The chorus of the birds rose with the sun.